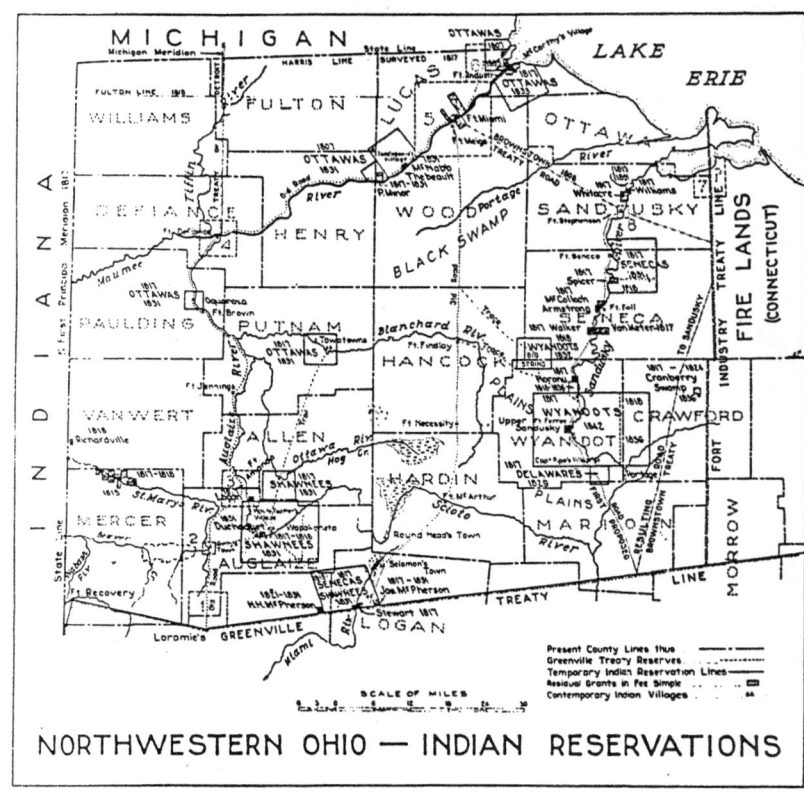

NORTHWESTERN OHIO — INDIAN RESERVATIONS

Main Treaties Ceding Indian Lands in Ohio

No.	Concluded	Place of Treaty	Acres Ceded	Tribes Concerned
1	1795, Aug. 3	Greenville, Ohio	16,930,417	Eleven northwestern tribes.
2	1805, July 4	Fort Industry, Ohio	2,726,812	Ottawas, Wyandots, Chippewas, Pottawatamies, Shawnees, Delawares.
3	1807, Nov. 17	Detroit, Michigan	345,600	Chippewas, Ottawas, Wyandots, Pottawatamies.
4	1808, Nov. 25	Brownstown, Mich.	Two roads	Same tribes as at Detroit.
5	1817, Sep. 29	Fort Meigs, Ohio	4,554,459	Same as at Fort Industry, and Senecas in addition.
6	1818, Sep. 17	St. Marys, Ohio		Ottawas, Shawnees, Wyandots and Senecas.
7	1818, Oct. 2	St. Marys, Ohio		Weas
8	1818, Oct. 6	St. Marys, Ohio	297,600	Miamis.

THE NATIVE TRIBES
OF
OLD OHIO

Helen Cox Tregillis

HERITAGE BOOKS
2007

HERITAGE BOOKS
AN IMPRINT OF HERITAGE BOOKS, INC.

Books, CDs, and more—Worldwide

For our listing of thousands of titles see our website
at
www.HeritageBooks.com

Published 2007 by
HERITAGE BOOKS, INC.
Publishing Division
65 East Main Street
Westminster, Maryland 21157-5026

Copyright © 1993 Helen Cox Tregillis

Other books by the author:

Illinois, the 14th Colony: French Period

People and Rural Schools of Shelby County, Illinois

Indians of Illinois

Ancestors: A Teaching Story Using the Families of Cox, Hayes, Hulse, Range, Worley and Others with Suggested Lessons

River Roads to Freedom: Fugitive Slave Notices and Sheriff Notices Found in Illinois Sources

Central Illinois Chronicles, Volumes 1-3

All rights reserved. No part of this book may be reproduced or transmitted in any form or by any means, electronic or mechanical, including photocopying, recording or by any information storage and retrieval system without written permission from the author, except for the inclusion of brief quotations in a review.

International Standard Book Number: 978-1-55613-925-X

TABLE OF CONTENTS
THE NATIVE TRIBES OF OLD OHIO

Map of Indian Reservations	Frontispage
Introduction	v
Manners & Customs of Ohio Tribes	1
The Mound Builders	14
The Eries	26
The Wyandots or Hurons	32
The Shawnees	40
The Senecas	47
The Delawares	54
The Miamis	58
The Ottawas	62
Villages & Trails	66
Biographies	71
World of the Great Spirit	91
Antecdotes & Other Stories	95
Early Blockhouses & Fortified Stations	99
Bibliography	105
Index	108

INTRODUCTION

Before 1492 the world was becoming smaller and smaller as different explorers searched out new lands. In the Americas, they encountered a rich variety of Native American tribes in the eastern forests of North America. Many Native Americans lived in farming villages near waterways. They supplemented cultivated crops -- corn, beans, melons and squash -- by hunting, fishing and gathering wild plants.

Native Americans of the northeast survived in many environments on lakeshores, in mountains and in forests. Some Algonquin tribes made homes in the Great Lakes area; others lived as far east as the Atlantic. French and English forces -- competing for land and furs -- took advantage of rivalries between the many Algonquin tribes.

Native Americans of the eastern woodlands taught early settlers many things about living in the new world. They showed the newcomers the variety of crops first domesticated by them: corn, beans, squash, pumpkins and tobacco. And they introduced such items as canoes, moccasins and snowshoes. Native American place names are prevalent in North America, and Native American words such as squash, moose and hickory are common.

About 1000 BC forest people of the Ohio valley began building burial mounds by heaping basketloads of earth over the log-lined tombs of their elite. Their culture, called Adena, was also marked by cord-or-fabric impressed pottery, and perhaps, even at this early date, by some plant cultivation. The Adena believed in an afterlife and used an art of stylized animal forms, and much of this same culture was expressed in the Hopewell culture which replaced Adena in the Ohio Valley beginning about 300 BC.

In addition to burial mounds, typical Hopewell finds include extensive geometrical earth works, remains of cremated dead, and an astonishing range of tomb-offerings. The obsidian, sheet mica, copper, pearls and other imported materials used in Hopewell mortuary art reached the Ohio Valley through a remarkable trade network that stretched from the Rockies to the Atlantic and from the Great Lakes to the Gulf Coast.

Though Hopewell culture and influence had disappeared by 700 AD, its basic subsistance pattern of forest hunting and farming continued over most of the northeast until European contact more than eight centuries later.

The state of Ohio became a melting pot for many Native American tribes as colonists pushed on from the east and south. This story that follows is intended to inform the general public of the rich history of the Native American.

The battle line was drawn -- north of the Ohio was to be the lands of the Native Americans -- to the south and east -- the new Americans. Tecumseh's dream of this reality never materialized. The War of 1812 shattered the possibility of a united Native American front.

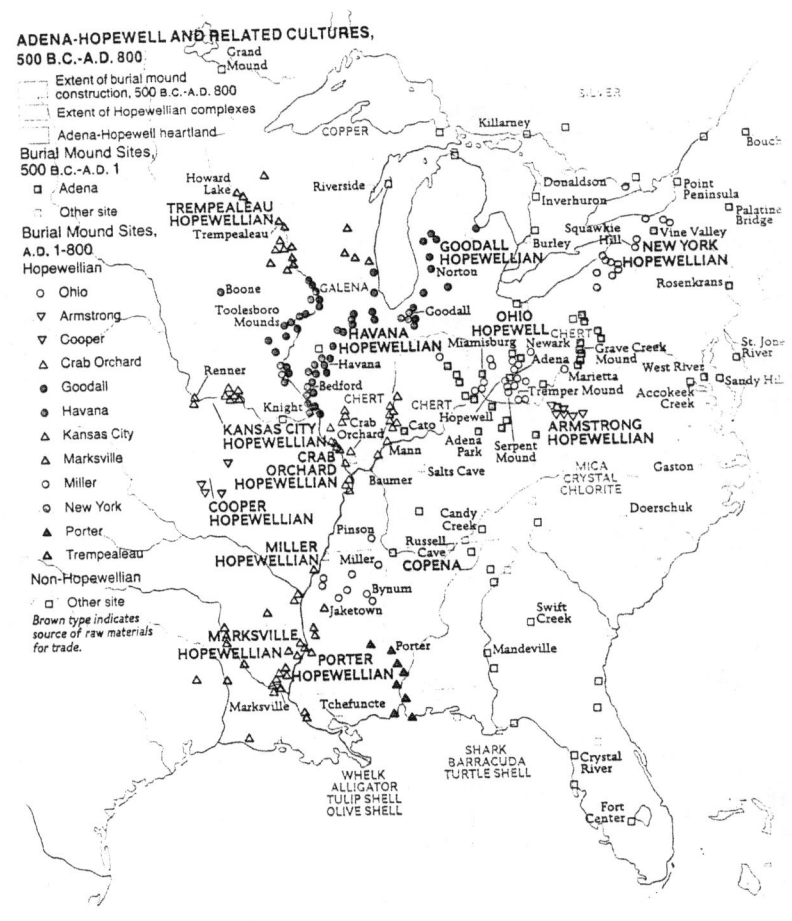

MANNERS AND CUSTOMS OF OHIO TRIBES
CHAPTER ONE

The customs and manners and lifestyles were similar among all the tribes of the Ohio territory as the new settlers found them. Living sites selected were free from timber, and a place where the canoes could be easily landed, and the women could have easy access to water. The strength of a village could be easily estimated, as lodges, wigwams and cabins were invariably placed in one line along the stream; some of the towns extended thus for two or three miles along the river.

The wigwams were constructed in a substantial way to resist wind and storm, and to keep the occupants comfortable through the winter season; some were large and roomy, twenty feet in diameter; others were smaller; circular or oval shaped, made of bark or matting laid over a frame work of poles that were stuck in the ground and leaning to the top, where an opening was left for the escape of smoke from the fire beneath. In the winter, these wigwams were also lined with matting, tastily made of rushes, grasses and reeds; bunks were made of poles, with skins and furs for bedding, the interior of the wigwam being cozily arranged and kept tidy and clean by the women; two openings were left on opposite sides, either to be used, according to the direction of the wind.

Cabins were arranged on the inside like the wigwams just described. The roofs were of bark or matting, and a hole was left in the center for the smoke to escape. A mat or skin was hung in the doorway. "Lodges" were not often found in the villages, being mostly used for temporary habitation in hunting camps, sugar camps and in the war camps that were sometimes formed as a base for operations at any great distance from the towns. Lodges were built in this way: A frame was formed by planting the ends of half hoops in the ground, the hoops one behind the other, about two feet apart. A ridge pole, or thong of hide, was fastened on top from bow to bow. Over the whole of it, matting or skins of wild animals were spread. The occupants slept on the ground, and the cooking being done in the open air.

Corn, beans, pumpkins and tobacco were the crops raised by the Indians. The tilled ground was not fenced. The animals were pastured at some distance from the villages to prevent injury to growing crops. By some of the tribes, fruit was also grown. The trees were seedlings grown from seed purchased of the traders. After the trading stations had been established in the west, the rude implements and tools used by the Indians were replaced with those better adapted to the cultivation of the soil, and for other domestic purposes. Steel traps took the place of "dead falls" and "pits." Awls and needles made of the bones of birds were no longer used in sewing garments and fitting the matting to the wigwams. Cultivation was accomplished with the iron hoe, and better cooking utensils were supplied.

The duties and toil of Indian life were the duties of the women. They built the wigwams and cabins, performed all the village drudgery and women's work, cared for dogs and ponies, gathered the fuel, planted the seed, cultivated the soil and harvested the crops, cut up and jerked the game brought in by the hunters, made the clothing, and when on journeys, carried great bundles of camp equipage.

The responsibility of the care of the families and wigwams was upon them. They were neat and tidy in their habits, and kept everything clean about the villages. They were uncomplaining and not quarrelsome. The women were not demonstrative, as a rule, but were thoroughly loyal to the family relations. Separations were of rare occurrece, but for cause, a husband might send his woman away.

Babies were not noisy. They were allowed to roll around the floor of the wigwam in cold or stormy weather, and in the open air during the milder seasons. To carry them about, they were slung to the woman's back. To leave them alone in the wigwams, they were bound to a board longer than themselves, and stood away in the corner. The younger children were never whipped, and were scarely ever scolded. Constant atttention was given to their training, that they might grow in experience to meet the necessities and ways of Indian life. They were taught to observe what they believed to be right. They were pointed to examples of bad Indians, and that such were despised by everybody. They were shown examples of braves, and honest Indians whom all respected, as worthy of imitation.

After boys were of hunting age, they were no longer under the government of the women, but were kept hunting all the time. From early spring until winter set in, they lived along the streams, learning to swim, to paddle canoes, to build canoes, to fish and trap. They roamed through the woods, learning to shoot and hunt, acquiring

the knowledge of woodcraft and the hardships of outdoor life. The young of both sexes developed early. At the age of 15, the boys were free to come and go without restraint. Two years younger than that, the girls were budding into womanhood, and it was a rare thing for a young woman to reach the age of 15 before being appropriated by some young man.

Courtship and marriage among the Indians were not attended with any very great delays or ceremony. When a man was attracted by the good features and figure of a handsome and tidy young woman, greased, painted and full feathered, in all the pomp and pride of a warrior, he would walk down the village street until, arriving before the wigwam of his intended, he stopped. Then, if his advances were at all encouraged, it was considered as an acceptance, and they were quickly paired. They were mated without being required to ask consent of any one, and without interference from any source. If the weather was favorable for outdoor enjoyment, a feast and dance would sometimes be arranged, in which old and young would participate, keeping up the merry-making until all were tired out. The Wyandots and Delawares prided themselves on their virtue and hospitality, and no authenticated case of the misuse of a female captive can be quoted. They always evinced the utmost modesty toward their female captives. Respect for the aged, for parents and those in authority prevailed. When one among them spoke, all listened, never, under any circumstances, interrupting him. When he was done, then was the time to reply.

In moving from one village to another, as families often did, the women, as under all other circumstances, had all the work to do. The wigwam goods were tied in great bundles and fastened on the backs of the ponies, or carried on the backs of the women, if there were not ponies enough. Riding or walking, the women carried the babies on their backs. Pelts were used in lieu of saddles, and man and woman rode alike -- straddle.

A halt was made for dinner, but the ponies were not unloaded except at night. There was but little trouble with the youngsters or babies. They were trained to be quiet, and rarely ever cried.

Upon arrival at the new location, it was the woman's duty to cut the poles and erect the wigwam, and arrange all for the comfort of her warrior. The interior of these wigwams were kept neat and clean, the sides lined with furs or matting for warmth. A cheerful fire blazing in the center made an attractive picture, as a place of shelter from any storm -- an abode of comfort. In going to bed, the men pulled off all clothing but their breechclouts, and the women all but the skirt. The clothing thus taken off was used for pillows.

Indian dress in the earlier times was exclusively made of furs and skins. Great taste was shown in making the garments, and in the arrangement of the ornaments used, such as shells, beads, and beautifully colored grasses and feathers. Indian tanned skins have always commanded the highest prices.

After the French occupation of the western country before 1750, cloth began to used by the women in making clothing for themselves and their youngsters. The brighter colors were the most popular -- anything so it was red, suited the Indian's fancy.

Warriors, old and young, were the most particular as to their personal appearance. Styles varied according to the tribal customs and identification when it came to men's hair. The breech-clout was a piece of linen, cloth or pelt, nearly a yard long, and eight or nine inches wide. This passed under the belt before and behind, leaving the ends to hand loosely over the belt. Leggins were made long to be fastened to the belt. The hips were thus left exposed.

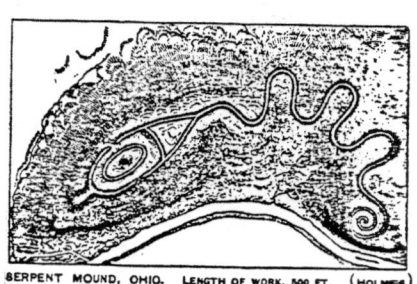

SERPENT MOUND, OHIO. LENGTH OF WORK, 500 FT. (HOLMES)

Moccasins covered the feet, and the ankles were closely wrapped. When expeditions to distant points were to be made, a fringed and ornamental shirt was worn to protect the body from the bushes. Thus dressed in the gorgeously colored deer-skin suit, wearing the wampum, with rifle, bullet-pouch and powder-horn, a glistening tomahawk and knife hanging in his belt, the warrior was ready for anything. Hunters, like the warriors, were dressed in full suits of deer-skin, but the decorations were not so profuse.

The women dressed in the gayest costumes their tastes could suggest, beautifully worked moccasins, soft deer-skin leggins, richly fringed and decorated in the brightess colors, with beads, shells and spangles. Pendants and necklaces were worn, strings of ornaments of bear's tusks and claws, stone medals and ear-rings. In the everyday village life, they wore an undergarment and skirt; in winter, furs were almost universally worn.

Whether man, woman or child, one act of cowardice or dishonesty was life-long disgrace to an Indian. Reverence and honor were paid to the aged, especially to parents. They were not quarrelsome or covetous. The sick were tenderly nursed, and the disabled properly cared for.

There was general pride in the skill of the hunters and achievements of the warriors. The return of a party from the war-path or from a hunting expedition, was always attended with public reception in the villages.

In the wigwams and villages, with the warriors and hunters, between the old and young, in all situations of life among the Indians, there was perfect equality. In their character and conduct were seen a strong sense of independence, a great aversion to anything that looked like caste or subjugation. They gloried in their native liberty, and for one of them to show a feeling of superiority was an effective barrier to all further success.

The chief of a tribe was not a ruler. He could neither make peace or war, and except as others were guided by his example, he had no control of affairs. A brave was chosen war chief upon his own merit as a warrior, as one of exceptional bravery and skill. The village chief was selected as one possessing administrative ability, of commanding address and great eloquence, well versed in the traditions of the tribe, and their relations to the neighboring tribes.

For purposes of consultation, and as a place to assemble the chiefs and braves, a council-house was usually built near the center of the village. There all met on an equality to determine questions of common interest. The council-house would be made of clapboards and poles, about 30 feet wide and 50 feet long. When the men entered the council-house, the women seated themselves on one side of the room, while the men occupied the opposite side. There was a small mound of earth in the center of the room, eight or ten feet in diameter, for the council fire. The ceremonies began with music made by beating on a small brass kettle, and on dried skins stretched over the mouths of pots. The pounding was accompanied by a chant. The group would be absolutely silent as they were addressed.

At the close of an address, dancing commenced. The men danced in files or lines by themselves around the central mound, the women following in a company by themselves. The Greentown tribes were always noted for being extremely scrupulous and modest in the presence of one another. After the dance, the refreshments, made by boiling venison and bear's meat together, were handed around.

They believed that the Great Spirit was Ruler over all, and that He was an Indian. Manitou was the name most generally given to the Great Spirit. The Indians believed that they were the first of the human race created; that they sprang from the brain of the Great Spirit; that they possessed all knowledge, and were under the special care of their Creator. Their traditions were vague, but their religious sentiments were clear. They had no fixed days or manners of worship. They believed in a future state of reward and punishment in the "happy hunting grounds" beyond the grave; that "all who do well will be happy, but those who do bad will be miserable."

The medicine men, who had care of the sick and were in charge of all religious feasts and observances, were held in great respect, as possessors of supernatural power. By the practice of their magic art, they were supposed to have close relations with the Great Spirit. Their medicines, made from roots and herbs, were, in their use, surrounded with all mystery possible. All the arts of the conjurer were solemnly practiced.

Indian burials were conducted with as much form as any of their ceremonies. In the grave with the corpse were buried the rifle and trappings of the warrior or hunter, his pipe and tobacco, and a sufficient quantity of parched corn or other provisions to last him on his journey to the happy hunting-grounds of the future life. There was no common place for the burial of the dead, each grave being located in the forests or on the hills, to suit the wishes of the surviving friends. When a man died or his woman died, the widower or widow would remain in mourning for about a year, after which being at liberty to mate again.

The regular times for feasts were when the green corn could first be used, in the hunting camps when the first game was killed, the war feast was celebrated after a victory, and there were great festivities in the villages upon the return of the warriors or of a hunting party. Notice of a feast was given by sending a runner to the wigwams with small pieces of decorated wood. The bearer would verbally give all particulars as to time and preparations. Men, women and the young would be seated on the ground around the fires, on which were boiling the kettles of green, juicy venison and bear meat, pots of fat coon and hominy. Men dressed for the trail, with waving plumes, military trappings and dangling decorations. Women wore bright-colored skirts and strings of flash-

ing ornaments, their black hair hanging in long braids, and babies rolling on the green sward, waiting for bowls of the rich mess. Each with wooden bowl and spoon would help themselves from the vessels. Then, with sugar or molasses as dressing, the abundant feast was enjoyed.

None but the warriors participated in the wild excitement of the war dance, but the young Indians were allowed to look on, as preparation for participation in later years. There were other dances that young and old joined with loud shoutings, and the clangor of tomtoms and other instruments. These dances were continued into the night, lighted by the blazing big fires.

The sports and pastimes of the Indians were in character more in the way of preparation and incentive to the objects and pursuits of Indian life, such as running races, jumping, wrestling, shooting, canoe races, throwing the tomahawk, practice with the bow and arrows. Football was a very popular game, the excitement sometimes lasting for several days, and involving the whole village in the sport.

The Miami Rivers, and the streams flowing into them, were favorite spawning and feeding waters for the choice varieties of the larger kind of fishes, and during the months of cool weather, many were taken by the Indians, in wicker traps and baskets, and by spearing. The young Indians had great sport in following the larger fish on the shoals and rapids, killing numbers with spears and arrows, and in the winter, through the ice, would spear many in the same way.

Trapping was the most profitable pursuit followed. Besides being a good school for the young Indians, it furnished employment for the villagers who were old, or who by accident or the fortunes of war were unable for more active duty. It sometimes happened, when the season was favorable and game unusually plentiful, that the whole tribe would devote the winter to the traps that were located at all favorable points along the streams, or occupy a stretch of country for 30 miles across the valleys.

The skins of muskrats, mink and other smaller animals were sought. Beaver, otter, coon and bear skins were more valuable, and all were in great demand at the trading stations north and east. The great abundance of game in the woods, the rich soil of the valleys of the northwest, in which were located the villages and cultivated lands of the Indians, were unfailing sources of supply.

Having the benefit of association with experienced

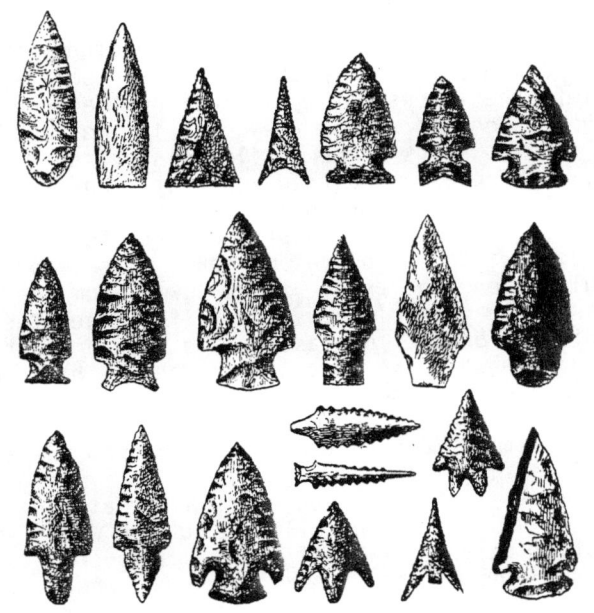
ARROW AND SPEAR HEADS.

skillful hunters on the different expeditions, Indian boys learned the mysteries of woodcraft and the wildlife ways. One great lesson learned was to be able to imitate notes and calls of the game birds, and the noise of the beasts of the forests. The turkey call, and harsher notes of wild duck and goose, would serve as a perfect decoy.

Of the animals hunted by the Native American, none seems to have elicited their skill more than the bear. To slay one of these beasts was proof of a warrior's prowess, and dangerous encounters often resulted in the hunter's search for such distinction. The vitality of bruin was unequaled among the animals of the forest, and because of the danger attached to his capture, he was made an object of special hunts and feats of courage.

The Black or Canesadooharaie River had always been famous among the tribes of Northern Ohio for the number and largeness of its bears. The habit of these animals was to search out a hollow tree or a warm clump of bushes late in the autumn, where they could remain three or four months, during the extreme cold of the winter, subsisting entirely on the fat of their bodies. They would emerge in spring very lean, and when so were exceedingly ferocious. When searching out their places of winter solitude, they often left the impress of their feet on the bark of the tree they ascended, or on the grass in the lair they had found. These signs were easily discovered by tribal hunters. The bears were then very fat, and were eagerly sought by the hunters for their flesh and fat. Sometimes they would ascend trees thirty or forty feet high, and find a good wintering place and take possession. Again they would ascend the tree, if hollow, from the inside, and, finding a good place, occupy it. Then the hunters would divide forces, one ascend the tree and with a long pole, sharpened at one end, or wrapped with a rag or dry skin saturated with grease and set on fire, thrust the same down on the bear and compel him to descend, only to meet his death at the foot of the tree from the arrow or bullet of the hunter below.

The skin of a fat bear was a great prize to a hunter. It made him an excellent couch on which to sleep, or a cloak to wear. His flesh was supposed to impart bravery to those who ate it, hence when dipped in sweetened bear's fat, it was considered an excellent dish and one often offered to friends. Venison, prepared the same way, was also considered a dish fit for the most royal visitors; a hospitality always extended to all who came to the camp, and if not accepted the donor was sure to be offended.

When war parties were sent out by the Shawnees, the Wyandots or the Miamis, or any of the tribes to the north of the Maumee, it was their custom, within a few days after their departure, to send as a re-enforcement or rather support in case of reverse and pursuit, a band of hunters, with women and camp equipage, to locate an advanced supply camp somewhere in the Miami or Scioto Valley. The party would come down the river in canoes to the mouth of the Mad River, Hole's Creek, Twin Creek or lower down at the head of Mill Creek, or at the mouth of either of the Miamis, where the lodges would be built.

Interpreters for the tribes were generally settlers who had been boy captives and had grown up with the Indians. Some of them were married to the women, reared families and acquired great influence over the tribes.

All the families, living in a long house or an equivalent group of houses, traces their descent from a common female ancestor. Each clan had its own name, usually that of some animal or bird, as the wolf, bear, turtle, eagle or turkey. Such animals or bird were held sacred, and carved images of them, called totems, served as kind of clan emblem, and were placed over the doors of their houses.

A certain number of clans, from three or four up to twenty or more, speaking the same language, constitute an Indian tribe. Every tribe, as a usual thing, elected a head war-chief and was governed by a council of its clan-sachems.

The cultivated products of the Ohio Indians exceeded in quantity those of any other equal area in North America. Many settlers and soldiers were always amazed at the huge stores of grain and large fields of corn found cultivated by the tribes.

When the season for planting drew near, the women cleared a spot of rich alluvial soil, and dug over the ground with their hoes. In planting the corn, they followed lines to a certain extent, thus forming rows each way across the field. When the corn began to grow, they

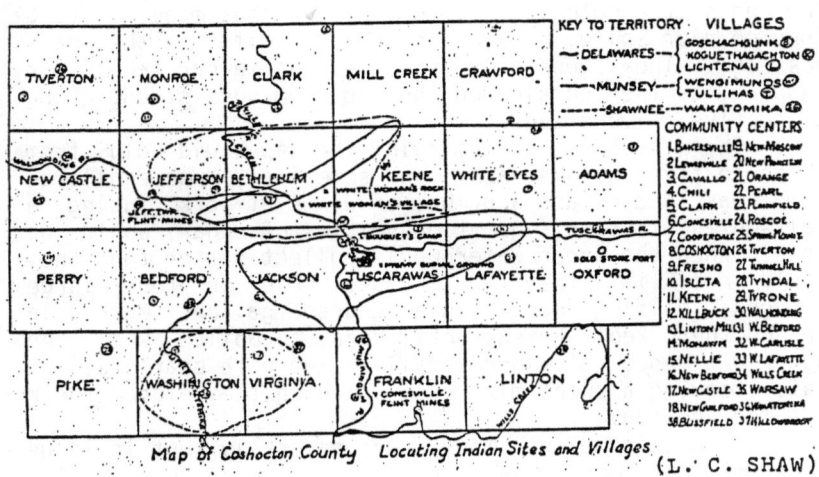

Map of Coshocton County Locating Indian Sites and Villages (L. C. SHAW)

cultivated it with wonderful industry until it had matured sufficiently for use. Their corn fields were nearly always in the vicinity of the villages, and sometimes were many acres in extent, and in favorable seasons yielded plentifully. The women raised the corn, dried it, pounded it into meal in a stone mortar, or made it into hominy. Corn in one form or another furnished the chief staple of the tribe's food. They had various legends concerning its origin, which, in common with other stories, they were accustomed to recite in their assemblies.

In the spring they made maple sugar by boiling the sap in large brass or iron kettles which they had obtained from the French and English traders. To secure the water they used vessels made of elm bark in a very ingenious manner.

They would strip the bark in the winter season, when it would strip or run, by cutting down the tree, and, with a crooked stick, sharp and broad at one end, peel the bark in wide strips, from which they would construct vessels holding two or three gallons each. They would often make over a hundred of these. They cut a sloping notch in the side of a sugar-tree, stuck a tomahawk into the wood at the end of the notch, and, in the dent thus made, drove a long chip or spile, which conveyed the water to the bark vessels. They generally selected the larger trees for tapping, as they considered the sap from such stronger and productive of more sugar.

Their vessels for carrying the sap would hold from three to five gallons each, and sometimes, where a large camp was located and a number of women at work, using a half-dozen kettles, great quantities of sugar would be made. When the sugar-water would collect faster than they could boil it, they would make three or four large troughs, holding more than a hundred gallons each, in which they kept the sap until ready to boil. When the sugar was made, it was generally mixed with bear's oil or fat, forming a sweet mixture into which they dipped their roasted venison.

The compound when made, was generally kept in large bags made of coon-skins, or vessels made of bark. The former were made by stripping the skin over the body toward the head, tying the holes made by the legs with buckskin cords, and sewing securely the holes of the eyes, ears and mouth.

The hair was all removed, and then the bag blown full of air, from a hole in the upper end, and allowed to dry. Bags made in this way would hold whisky, and were often used for such purposes. When they became saturated, they were blown full of air again, the hole plugged, and they were left to dry. Sometimes the head was cut off without stripping the skin from it, and the skin of the neck gathered in folds like a purse, below which a string was tied and fastened with a pin.

SCRAPERS—FLINT.

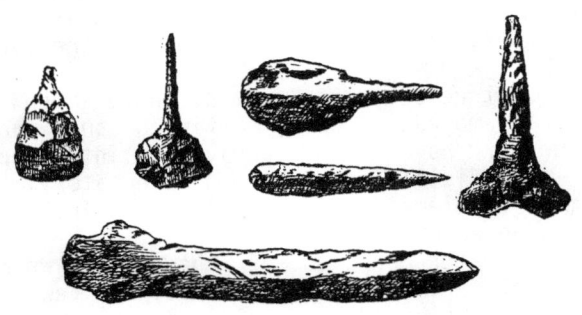

PERFORATORS—FLINT.

THE MOUND BUILDERS
CHAPTER TWO

The ancient works, commonly attributed to the Mound Builders, are spread over a large extent of country. They dot the valleys from the Alleghenies to the far northwest and extend from the lakes to the Gulf of Mexico.

The number of mounds in the state of Ohio may be safely estimated at ten thousand, and the number of enclosures at from one thousand to fifteen thousand. They are most numerous along the larger streams, and the seats of the most dense population of the ancient people seem to have been along the Ohio, the Scioto and the Miamis, although they are scattered more or less numerously over almost the whole state.

Not far from one hundred enclosures and five hundred mounds are found in Ross county, and along the fertile valley of the Scioto from the Ohio to Columbus it is safe to say there were at least three times this number of ancient remains.

All of these constructions are composed of earth or stone, and sometimes these materials are mixed, though rarely. In some instances the earth and stone composing these works are foreign in the locality, and must have been brought a considerable distance, but in the greater number of cases, it has been removed from the surrounding plain.

These structures, or mounds, have been properly divided into mounds proper, effigies and inclosures. Mounds proper have been subdivided into sepulchral, templar, sacrificial, memorial and observatory. Effigies are animal, emblematic and symbolical. Inclosures are military, covered or sacred.

The greater portion of the above works were constructed of earth, a few of stones, and fewer still of earth and stone combined. Sepulchral mounds are usually conical, and some of them, notwithstanding the lapse of time, are seventy feet in height. They are more numerous than any other class, and beyond doubt were erected as memorials to the dead. They always contained one or more skeletons, together with implements and ornaments supposed to have been placed when the individual was buried, for use in the Spirit Land.

The mounds are of all sizes, and it has been conjectured that their magnitude bears some relation to the prominence of the persons in whose honor they were erected. Ashes and charcoal are often found in proximity to the skeletons, under conditions which render it probable that fires were used in the burial ceremony. With the skeletons are also found specimens of mica, pottery, bone and copper beads, and animal bones. Though in this class of mounds, ordinarily but one skeleton is found, yet sometimes several are unearthed.

A few years before 1880, a mound, situated in Licking County, was opened, and found to contain, in whole or in part, seventeen skeletons. But the most noteworthy of the mounds was one in Hardin County, which contained 300 crumbling skeletons.

Templar mounds are few in number, and are ordinarily circular. They are invariably truncated, and are often surrounded with embankments, inclined planes or spiral pathways or steps, leading to the summit. They are found round, square, oblong, oval and octangular, and rest generally on a large base, but have a limited altitude. It was supposed that these elevations were surmounted with wooden temples, all traces of which have been removed by the ravages of time.

These mounds and buildings at their summits are thought to have been erected for religious purposes. Sacrificial mounds are ordinarily stratified, with convex layers of clay and loam above a stratum of sand. They usually contain ashes, charcoal, igneous stone, calcined animal bones, beads, stone implements, pottery and specimens of sculpture.

They are often found within inclosures, which are supposed to have been connected with the religious ceremonies of the Mound Builders. Altars of igneous clay or stone are often found. Evidences of fire upon the altars yet remain, showing that various animals and probably human beings were immolated to secure the favor of the Great Spirit.

These mounds infrequently contain skeletons, together with implements of war; mica from the Alleghanies; shells from the Gulf of Mexico; differently colored varieties of obsidian; red, purple and green specimens of porphyry; and silver, copper and other metallic ornaments and utensils.

Mounds of observation were apparently designed for alarm-towers or signal stations. They are often found built like towers from the summits of embankments surrounding inclosures. One of the latter, in Licking County, has a height of 25 feet. Along the Miami River are dotted small mounds or projecting highlands, which

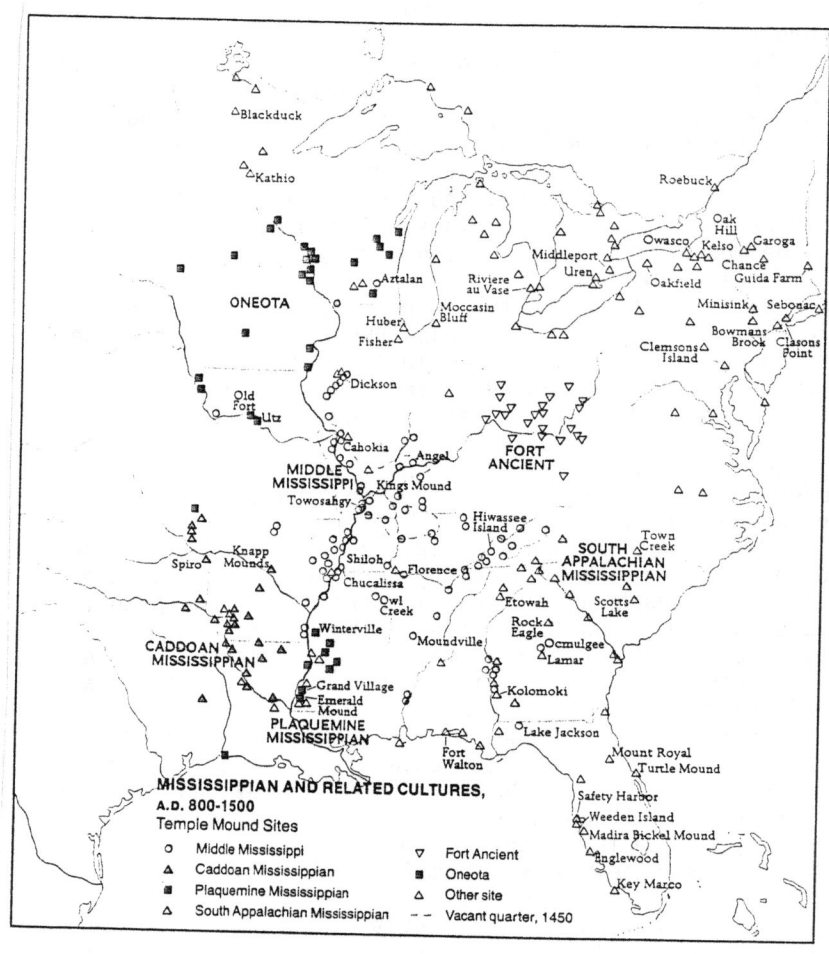

seem to have been built to carry intelligence by signals along the valley.

Memorial mounds are of that class of tumuli intended to commemorate some important event, or to perpetuate the memory of some distinguished character. Most of the stone mounds belong to this class, and usually contain no bones, for the supposed reason that they were used only for sepulchers.

Effigies are elevations of earth in the form of men, beasts, bird, reptiles and occasionally, of inanimate objects, varying in height from one foot to six foot above the surrounding soil, and often covering many acres of land. Some believe that these were erected in accordance with the religious beliefs who worshiped, or in some way venerated, the animals or objects represented by the elevations.

A large mound near Newark represents a bird of enormous size, with its wings outspread in the act of flight. Its total length is about 200 feet. An excavation in this effigy disclosed a clay and stone altar, upon which were evidences of fire, together with ashes and charcoal. This mound being called the "Eagle Mound."

Another mound near Newark represents a huge alligator, having a total length of 200 feet. The greatest breadth of the body is twenty feet, and its body from hind legs to fore legs is fifty feet. Each limb is twenty-five feet long. The principal portions of the animal are elevated about six feet, while other portions are much lower.

The most remarkable mound in Ohio is in Adams County. Its form is that of an enormous serpent, more than a thousand feet in length with body in graceful, anfractuos folds, and tail ending in triple coils. The greatest width of the body is 30 feet, and the effigy is elevated about five feet above the surrounding soil. The neck of the figure is stretched out and slightly curved, and the mouth is opened wide, as if in the act of swallowing or ejecting an oval figure, which rests partly within the distended jaws. Some feel this is similar to the idea of the serpent and the egg.

Defensive inclosures are irregular in form, and are always on high ground, in positions difficult to approach by a savage foe. The walls generally wind around the borders of the elevations they occupy, and when the nature of the ground renders some points more accessible than others, the height of the wall and the depth of the ditch

at these weak points are proportionally increased. The gateways are narrow and few in number, and well guarded by embankments of earth placed a few yards inside of the openings or gateways, and parallel with them at each end, thus fully covering the entrances, which, in some cases, are still further protected by projecting walls on either side.

These works are somewhat numerous, and indicate a clear appreciation of, at least, the elements of fortification, and unmistakably point out the purpose for which they were constructed. A large number of these defensive works consist of a line of ditches and embankments, or several lines, carried across the neck of peninsulas or bluff headlands, formed within the bends of streams.

The embankments of one of this class in Warren County are nearly four miles in length, varying in height from ten to twenty feet to accord with the locality to be protected, and inclose several hundred acres. Covered ways or parallel walls are often found, either connecting different inclosures or portions of the same. They were undoubtedly designed to protect those passing back and forth within.

There are large numbers of sacred inclosures in the form of circles, squares, hexagons, octagons, ellipses, parallelograms and others, many of which were designed with geometrical accuracy. They are sometimes found within military inclosures, and very likely were connected with the religious rites and ceremonies of the people, as small elevations are found within them, which were evidently used for altars.

GREAT EARTH-WORK NEAR NEWARK.

The section of the Scioto River valley contained within the county of Ross and the Paint creek area had the densest population of the Mound Builders. Chillicothe is the central point of ten groups of large works: four have two and a half miles of enbankment each, and two of them enclose an area of a hundred acres apiece, while the others have different areas.

Many of the mounds held altars and human remains, broken pottery, implements, shells and other objects. One of the most perfect skulls found in the mounds exhibited a facial angle of 81 degrees, and was of unusually large size -- larger than the Mongolian, Caucasian or American Indian skulls.

About a mile southeast of Miamisburg, Montgomery County, in 1869, a shaft was dug in the a large mound revealing a human skelton in a sitting position, facing due east, at eight feet from the top. A deposit of vegetable matter, bones of small animals, also wood and stone, were surrounding the skeleton, while a cover of clay several feet in thickness, with a layer of ashes and charcoal, seems to have been the burial. At the depth of 24 feet was discovered a triangular stone planted perpendicularly in the earth, with the point upward. Around this stone at an angle of 45 degrees, and overlapping each other like the shingles upon a roof, were placed rough stones averaging about one foot in diameter, of nearly uniform size, and similar to those quarried in the neighboring hills.

Before 1868 when the Ohio canal was dug for the Licking Summit Reservoir, a stone and earth pyramid was dismantled near Newark. Beneath the truncated circular pyramid was found a hollowed oak log coffin and a stone relic exhibiting Hebrew writing.

The coffin was lined with a fabric resembling old carpeting, so fragile that it crumbled at the slightest touch. On this the body of the deceased was laid. Among the skeleton remains were black locks of hair and ten copper rings. The whole was embedded in clay, over which was an arch of small and large stones. The whole enclosure over the coffin about seven feet in height.

Rev. J.W. M'Carty of Newark, a Hebrew scholar, translated the words on three of the four sides of the stone as follows: Holy of Holies, The Word of the Law, and The Word of the Lord. The stone was in; the form of a truncated cone, five inches in length, with two sides broader than the other two sides, and a neck and knob, evidently formed for suspending it by a cord or chain. It had the

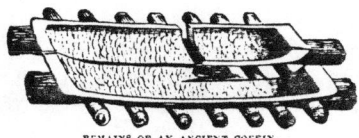

REMAINS OF AN ANCIENT COFFIN.

THE FOUR SIDES OF THE HOLY STONE.

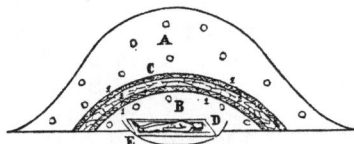

SECTIONAL VIEW OF THE PYRAMID.

STONE AXES.

John Johnston

appearance of a hone-stone and was finely polished.

In January 1881 in Madison County near Deek Creek, two skeletons were found in a mound about 240 feet at the base and about 12 feet in height. The different layers of burnt clay, charcoal and ashes being the same as in all mounds. Other mounds can be found in the county.

The largest mound in Madison County is classified as a temple mound being about 600 feet around the base and about 25 feet in height. During the pioneer days of Ohio, the Indians used the area as a favorite camping ground and as a favorite burial place.

About 1867 investigations were made of the mound builders remains in Clinton County, Ohio. Many of their findings were finished slate relics and copper implements that were given to the Smithsonian.

Until the turn of the century, few of the mounds were opened in Richland County. In most of the places the plow had changed the original formations. Very few, if any, copper implements were found here.

The most noteworthy of the mounds was one found in Hardin County which contained 300 crumbling skeletons.

Another mound discovered in Summit County in 1843 when an addition was made to a canal revealed 30 to 40 skeletons lying in irregular rows, extending north and south, with some heads to the east and some to the west. There were skeletons of males and females and perhaps one-third were children. A stone kettle, four inches deep and eight inches across was found in one of the graves.

What is known as the Hopetown group of works is situated four miles north of Chillicothe, on the east bank of the Scioto. These works consist of a circle and in conjunction therewith a much more important inclosure which appears at first glance to be a rectangle, though in reality it is an irregular octagon.

The circle extends in to the octagonal inclosure, instead of being connected in the usual manner. The octagonal inclosure measures nine hundred by nine hundred and fifty feet, and the diameter of the circle is one thousand and fifty feet.

The walls of the circle are now very slight, but, although cultivated for many years, can be easily traced, at least in 1880. They were never more than three or four feet in height.

Mound City is in many respects the most remarkable of works in the Scioto Valley. It is situated upon the western bank of the Scioto, and between three and four miles north of Chillicothe. In outline the inclosure is nearly square, with rounded corners, and consists of a simple wall, about three feet high. Its site is the level of the second terrace. The area of the inclosure is thirteen acres. Within the wall there are twenty-four mounds, nearly all of which were excavated previous to 1846.

The implements made and used by these people has revealed their character. Very few copper implements have been found since if left on the surface, they soon disappeared by decomposition. Articles of bronze and brass are not found with the builders of the mounds.

Stone relics are very numerous and well preserved. Stone axes, mauls, hammers, chisels, etc., are very plentiful. None were made with holes or eyes for the insertion of a helve or handle but all wrought stones had a groove to receive a withe twisted into the form of a handle.

Axes were made more perfect by rubbing and polishing, probably done from time to time after they were brought into use. Double-headed hammers have the groove in the middle. They were made of the same material as the axes.

Implements, known as "fleshers" and "skinners", chisel-formed, commonly called "celts," were probably used as aids in peeling the skins of animals from the meat and bones.

Stone pestles are not plentiful while stone mortars are rare, indicating that they were made of wood, which is lighter and more easily transported. Most of the pestles are short, with a wide base, tapering toward the top. They were probably used with one hand, and moved about in the mortar in a circle.

There is almost an endless variety of perforated plates, thread-sizers, shuttles, etc. They are usually made of striped slate, most of which have tapering holes through them flatwise.

A great variety of wands or badges of distinction are found. They are nearly all fabricated from striped and variegated slate, highly finished, very symmetrical and elegant in proportion, evidently designed to be ornamental.

Arrow and spear heads and other similar pieces of flaked flint are the most abundant of any of the relics. A classification of the arrow-heads is rarely attempted. Spear-heads exhibit as a large a variety as arrow-heads, and like the latter, were inserted in wooden handles of various lengths, though in many tribes they were fastened

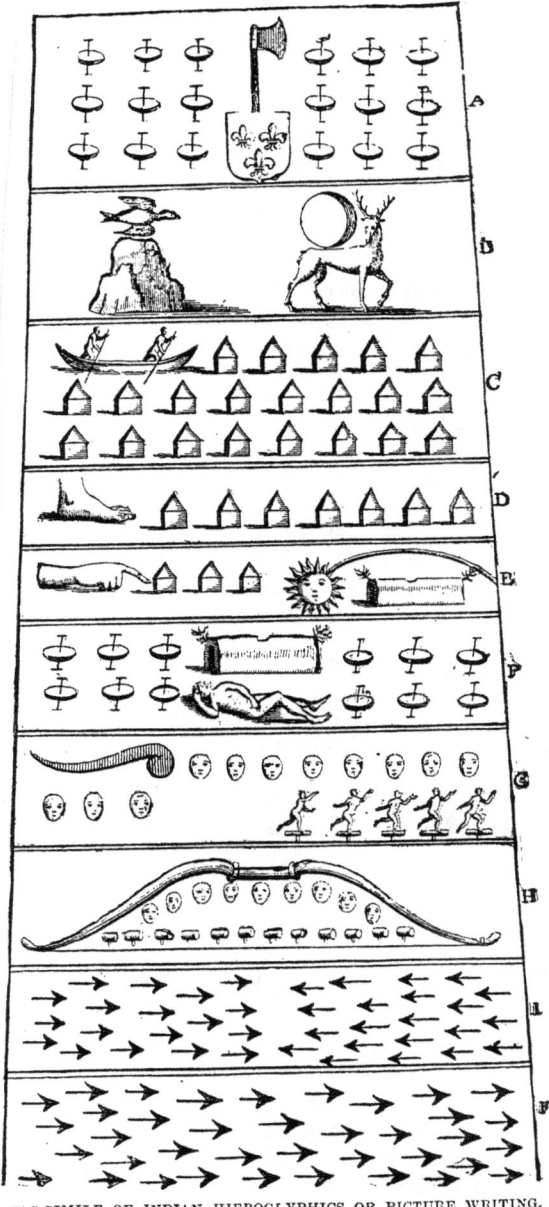

FAC-SIMILE OF INDIAN HIEROGLYPHICS OR PICTURE WRITING.
(From La Hontan, 1689.)

by thongs of untanned leather or sinews.

Theirs modes of manufacture were generally the same. Sometimes tribes contained arrow-makers, whose business was to make these implements, selling them to or exchanging them with their neighbors for wampum or peltries.

When the individual desired an arrow or spear head, he could buy one of the arrow-maker or make one himself. The common method was to take a chipping implement, generally made of the pointed rods of a deer's horn, from eight to sixteen inches in length, or of slender, short pieces of the same material, bound with sinews to wooden sticks resembling arrow-shafts. The arrow-maker held in his left hand the flake of flint or obsidian on which he intended to operate, and pressing the point of the tool against its edge, detached scale after scale, with much ingenuity, until the flake assumed the desired form.

It may be conjectured from many historical facts that the Mound Builders were a foreign people who invaded the soil of this continent. It is a well-known historical fact that the northmen reached the coast of North America from Greenland in 999, and from this it is theorized, that, perhaps the mysterious Mound Builders were no other than these.

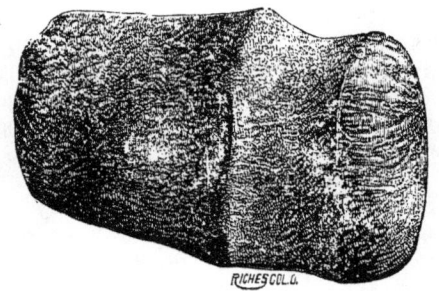

HEAVY STONE AXE.

THE ERIES
CHAPTER THREE

Before 1655 the Eries, a member of the Iroquois family, inhabited the land on the south shores of the lake which received their name. How big their area was is not known. They inhabited the territory extending south from Lake Erie to the Ohio River, east to the lands of the Conestoga along the east watershed of the Allegheny River and to those of the Seneca along the line of the west watershed of the Genesee River and north to those of the Neutral Nation, probably on a line running east from the head of the Niagara River and west to the west watershed of Lake Erie and Miami River to the Ohio River.

The Erie had many sedentary towns and vilages, that they were constituted of several divisions, and that they cultivated the soil and spoke a language resembling that of the Hurons.

As early as 1605, according to Louis Hennepin, Charlevois and other French historians, the Six Nations of Mohawks, Oneidas, Onondagas, Cayugas, Senecas and Tuscaroras formed an alliance so powerful that they began enlarging their territory by conquest.

At the taking of the Erie town of Rique in 1654, the defenders numbered between 3,000 and 4,000 combatants, exclusive of women and children, but as it is not likely that all the warriors of the tribe were present, 14,500 would probably be a conservative estimate of the population of the Erie at this time.

In 1654 some Hurons sought asylum among the Eries, and that it was they who were actively fomenting the war that was then striking terror among the Iroquois tribes. The Eries were reputed fiece and warlike, employing only bows and poisoned arrows.

Earlier in 1653 the Erie assaulted and burned a Seneca town, pursued an Iroquois war party returning from the region of the Great Lakes, and cut to pieces its rear guard of 80 picked men, while the Erie scouts had come to the very gate of the Iroquois palisaded town and seized and carried into captivity Annenraes, one of the greatest captains.

All this aroused the Iroquois tribes, which raised 1800 men to chastise the Eries. The Eries regarded the situation with the greatest apprehension. Never doubting the personal superiority of their warriors, they dreaded the power of the allied tribes on account of overwhelming numbers. The destruction of the Wyandots or Hurons was suggestive of the possibility of their fate, however the character and disposition of the confederate warriors was unknown. It was resolved to put them to the test.

To cope with them collectively they saw was impossible. Their only hope, therefore, was in being able by a vigorous and sudden movement to destroy them in detail. With this view a powerful party was immediately organized to attack the Senecas, who resided at the foot of Seneca Lake (the present site of Geneva) and along the banks of Seneca River.

It happened at this time period there resided among the Eries, a Seneca woman who in early life had been taken a prisoner and had married a husband of the Erie tribe. He died and left her a widow without children, a stranger among strangers. Hearing the terrible note of preparation for a bloody onslaught upon her kindred and friends, she formed the resolution of apprising them of their danger.

As soon as night set in, taking the course of the Niagara River, she traveled all night, and early next morning reached the shores of Lake Ontario. She jumped into a canoe, which she found fastened to a tree, and boldly pushed into the open lake.

Coasting down the lake, she arrived at the mouth of the Oswego River in the night, where a large settlement of the nation resided. She directed her steps to the house of the head chief, and disclosed the object of her journey. She was secreted by the chief, and runners were dispatched to all the tribes, summoning them immediately to meet in council, which was held in Onondaga hollow.

When all were convened, the chief arose, and in the most solemn manner rehearsed a vision, in which he said that a beautiful bird appeared to him and told him that a great party of the Eries was preparing to make a secret and sudden descent upon them to destroy them, and that nothing could save them but an immediate rally of all the warriors of the Five Nations, to meet the enemy before they should be able to strike the blow.

These solemn announcements were heard in breathless silence. When the chief had finished and sat down there arose one immense yell of menacing madness. The earth shook when the might mass brandished high in air their war-clubs, and stamped the ground like furious beasts.

No time was lost. A body of five thousand warriors was organized, and a corps of reserve, consisting of one thousand young men who had never been in battle. The bravest chiefs of all the tribes were put in command, and spies immediately sent out in search of the enemy, the whole body taking up their line of march in the direction whence they expected the attack.

The advance of the party was continued several days, passing through, successively, the settlements of their friends, the Onondagas, the Cayugas and the Senecas; but they had scarcely passed the last wigwam, now the fort of Canandaigua lake, when the scouts brought in intelligence of the advance of the Eries, who had already crossed the Genesee river in great force. The Eries had not the slightest intimation of the approach of their enemies. They relied on the secrecy and celerity of their movements to surprise and subdue the Senecas almost without resistance.

The two parties met at a point aboaut half way between the foot of Canandaigua lake, on the Genesee river, and near the outlet of two small lakes, near the foot of one of which Honeoye the battle was fought. When the two parties came in sight of each other, the outlet of the lake only intervened between them.

The entire force of the five confederate tribes was not in view of the Eries. The reserve corps of one thousand young men had not been allowed to advance in sight of the enemy. Nothing could resist the impetuosity of the Eries at the first sight of an opposing force on the other side of the stream.

They rushed through it and fell upon them with tremendous fury. The undaunted courage and determined bravery of the Iroquois could not avail against such a terrible onslaught, and they were compelled to yield the

TOTEMS.

FAC-SIMILE FROM LA HONTAN—1703.

ground on the bend of the stream. The whole force of the combined tribes, except the corps of the reserve, now became engaged. They fought hand to hand and foot to foot. The battle raged horribly. No quarter was asked or given on either side.

As the fight thickened and became more desperate, the Eries, for the first time, became sensible of their true situation. What they had long anticipated had become a fearful reality. Their enemies had combined for their destruction, and they now found themselves engaged, suddenly and unexpectedly, in a struggle not only involving the glory, but perhaps the very existence of their nation.

They were proud, and had heretofore been victorious over all their enemies. Their superiority was felt and acknowledged by all the tribes. They knew how to conquer, but not to yield. All these considerations flashed upon the minds of the bold Eries, and nerved every arm with almost super-human power. On the other hand, the united forces of the weaker tribes, now made strong by union, fired with a spirit of emulation, excited to the highest pitch among the warriors of the different tribes, brought for the first time to act in concert, inspired with zeal and confidence by the counsels of the wisest chiefs, and led by the most experienced warriors of all the tribes, the Iroquois was invincible.

Though staggered by the first desperate rush of their opponents, they rallied at once, and stood their ground. And now the din of battle rises higher; the war-club, the tomahawk, the scalping knife, wielded by herculean hands, do terrible deeds of death. During the hottest of the battle, which was fierce and long, the corps of reserves, consisting of a thousand young men, were by skillful movement under their experienced chief, placed in the rear of the Eries, on the opposite side of the stream, in ambush.

The Eries had been driven seven times across the stream, and had as often regained their ground; but the eighth time, at a given signal from their chief, the corps of young warriors in ambush rushed upon the almost exhausted Eries with a tremendous yell, and at once decided the fortunes of the day.

Hundreds, disdaining to fly, were struck down by the war-clubs of the vigorous young warriors, whose thirst for the blood of the enemy knew no bounds. A few of the vanquished Eries escaped to carry the news of the terrible overthrow to their wives and children and old men that remained at home. But the victors did not allow them a moment's repose, but pursued them in their flight, killing all who fell in their hands.

Two Iroquois chiefs dressed as Frenchmen in order to frighten the Erie by the novelty of their garments. When the arm of invaders surrounded the Erie town of Rique, one of the chiefs gently asked the besieged to surrender, lest they be destroyed should they permit an assault, telling them: "The Master of Life fights for us; you will be ruined if you resist him."

"Who is this Master of our lives?" the Eries defiantly replied. "We acknowledge none but our arms and hatchets."

No quarter was asked or given on either side in this war. After a stubborn resistance, the Erie palisade was overtaken.

This devastating war lasted until about the close of 1656, when the Erie power was broken and the people were destroyed or dispersed or led into captivity.

Six hundred surrendered at one time and were led to the Iroquois country to be adopted as one of the constituent people of the Iroquois tribes.

The Iroquois remained in the enemy's country two months to care for the wounded and to bury the dead.

Only two of the Erie villages are known by name -- Rique and Gentaienton. A portion of the so-called Seneca now living in Indian territory are probably descendants of the Erie refugees.

IROQUOIS DRUM.

31

THE WYANDOTS OR HURONS
CHAPTER FOUR

January 21, 1785 Treaty with the Wyandot, Delaware, Chippewa, and Ottawa. Boundaries established between these Wyandot and Delaware tribes in Ohio. Certain reserves created for them.

August 3, 1795 Treaty with the Wyandot, Delaware, Shawnee, Ottawa, Chippewa, Potawatomi, Miami, Eel-river, Wea, Kickapoo, Piankashaw and Kaskaskia. New boundaries established in Ohio. Earlier treaties deemed null and void.

July 4, 1805 Treaty with the Wyandot, Ottawa, Chippewa, Munsee, Delaware, Shawnee and Potawatomi. A new boundary line established between tribal lands and those of the United States.

September 29, 1817 Treaty with the Wyandot, Seneca, Delaware, Shawnee, Potawatomi, Ottawa and Chippewa. Smaller tracts of Ohio land granted to tribes and certain individuals.

September 17, 1818 Treaty with the Wyandot, Seneca, Shawnee and Ottawa. Grants given in the treaty of 1817 to be considered only as reservations for the use of the tribes. Additional tracts granted to the Wyandot, Shawnee, and Seneca.

January 19, 1832 Treaty with the Wyandot. Tribe ceded to the United States their tract of land at the Big Spring, Crawford County, Ohio. This group had separated from Wyandots at Upper Sandusky. They could choose to move to Canada or the river Huron in Michigan to land they owned.

March 17, 1842 Treaty with the Wyandot. Tracts remaining in Ohio and Michigan to be ceeded to United States in exchange for land west of the Mississippi. Certain individuals receive grants in fee simple.

The French called this group Huron because of the way they wore their hair -- bristled like a boar. However, the group called themselves Wendat. They planted large varieties of several kinds of corn, squashes, tobacco, many varieties of beans, and sunflowers from which they made an oil for their hair. Their towns or villages were permanent, only changing location when the fields wore out.

The Wyandots or Hurons, who, at the time the French missionaries came to America were dwelling in the peninsula of Michigan, were allowed by the Five Nations to occupy the land of the Eries, and thus came to dwell in Ohio.

From Howe's Historical Collections, it ascertained that the Wyandots once occupied the north site of the St. Lawrence then down to Coon lake, and from thence up the Ottawas. The Senecas owned the opposite side of the river, and the island upon which Montreal now stands. Both were large tribes, consisting of many thousands, and were blood relations, claiming each other as cousins.

A war originated between the two tribes in the following manner: A wyandot brave wanted a certain woman for his wife; she objected; said he was no warrior, as he had never taken any scalps. He then raised a party of warriors and they set upon a small party of Senecas, killing and scaping a number of them.

It is presumed that the Wyandot brave secured his wife, but this created a war between the tribes which lasted more than a hundred years, and until both nations were much weakened, and the Wyandots nearly exterminated. The latter were compelled to leave the country, and took up their residence on the peninsula of Michigan, as before stated. They were often compelled to fight their old enemies even in this far off region, and war parties of Senecas frequently went there for that purpose. A peace was finally arranged, and the remnant of Wyandots came to reside in Ohio.

In 1745 a considerable party of Hurons or Wyandots under the leadership of the war chief Orontony or Nicholas removed from the Detroit river to the marsh lands of Sandusky bay. The French destroyed his villages in April 1748 at Sandusky, and forced the chief with 119 warriors and their families to flee to White river, Indiana. The chief died that same autumn thus ending the troubles with the French.

After this trouble the Hurons seem to have returned to Detroit and Sandusky, where they became known as Wyandots and gradually acquired a paramount influence in the

Ohio valley and the lake region. They laid claim to the greater part of Ohio, and the settlement of the Shawnees and Delawares within that area was with their consent; they exercised the right to light the council fire at all intertribal councils.

The Wyandots had three villages on the Scioto, in the vicinity of the site of Columbus. They were among the bravest of the Indian tribes, and flight in battle was by them considered disgraceful, even when fighting at a disadvantage. In 1774, a skirmish took place near the site of Columbus, between a party of soldiers belonging to Lord Dunmore's army, under the command of Col. William Crawford, and a band of Indians who were pursued to this point, here overtaken and defeated. It was from Darby, a chief of the Wyandot nation, who lived near the site of Plain City, that the largest stream in Madison County took its name.

In 1781 the chief of the Wyandots was Half King, and two Indians engaged with Adam and Andrew Poe were Half King's sons, but neither was a chief. Three of the Indians in the raiding party, as before stated, were sons of Half King, one of whom was the leader, named Scotash. The latter was wounded in his hand, and was the only one who escaped and returned to his tribe to tell the fate of his brothers and companions. The encounter was a desperate one from the fact that Poe grappled with both of them, and before he succeeded in killing the smaller Indian, he had been severely wounded in the wrist by a blow from his tomahawk.

It is stated that Scotash, the warrior who escaped from the terrific combat, made his way to the Wyandot town near Upper Sandusky, crossing the Tuscarawas on the trail about Fort Laurens, and before entering the Wyandot town, announced his coming by a series of dismal howls, which indicated that the expedition had been defeated and his brothers killed. This solitary survivor remained in the woods a whole day giving vent to his grief by moaning and howling alternately. The whole Wyandot tribe long mourned the loss of the sons of the Half King.

It is also stated that when they received the news of this disastrous defeat their indignation knew no bounds, and that they at once put to death a number of prisoners then in their hands. Among these who were spared was a young man named George Folks. He owed his life to a young woman who had fallen in love with him and procured his return home, near Darlington, Beaver county, Pa., where he lived to an old age. In after years two young women from the Wyandot reservation made him a visit, and received many presents to take home.

Many of the facts connected with this affair are obtained from the manuscript account by Thomas Edington of his captivity with the Wyandots. He was finally released and returned home after two years captivity. Mr. Edington was the father of Jess Edington who resided in Brooke County, Virginia nearly opposite Steubenville.

On 21 January 1785 at Fort M'Intosh, the Wyandots along with the Delawares, Chippewas, and Ottawas, signed a treaty with the United States, establishing the boundary line between the stated different tribes. Ten years later another treaty had to be established to settle controversy over boundaries. This later treaty made all others before it null and void.

Signing this treaty at Greenville, Ohio were Wyandots: Tarhe or Crane, J. Williams Jr., Teyyaghtaw, Haroenyou or Half King's son, Tehaawtorens, Awmeyeeray, Stayetah, Shateyyaronyah or Leather Lips, Daughshuttayah and Shaawrunthe.

On the fourth of July 1805, the Wyandots again were involved in a treaty at Fort Industry. Signing this treaty for the Wyandots were: Tarhee or Crane, Miere or Walk in Water, Thateyyanayoh or Leather Lips, Harrowenyou or Cherokee Boy, Tschauendah, Tahunehawettee or Adam Brown and Shawrunthie.

Three years later at Detroit, only three Wyandot chiefs affixed their signature to the treaty: Skahomet, Miere or Walk in Water and Iyonayotha.

Many of the same chiefs signed the treaty in 1808 at Brownstown, Michigan: Miere or Walk in Water, Iyonayotaha or Joe, Skahomet or Black Chief and Adam Brown.

In 1817 on the Miami of Lake Erie, a treaty with the Wyandots established firmer boundaries for them on the Upper Sandusky, a tract of land twelve miles square. Those chiefs at that time being: Doanquod, Howoner, Rontondee, Tauyau, Rontayau, Dawatont, Manocue, Tauyaudautauson and Haudaunwaugh.

Other patents in fee simple were granted to Wyandots related by blood or adoption. Quoting from that treaty of 1817:

"To Elizabeth Whitaker, who was taken prisoner by the Wyandots, and has ever since lived among them, 1280 acres of land, on the west side of the Sandusky River, below Croghansville, to be laid off in a square from, as nearly as the meanders of the said river will admit, and to run an equal distance above and below the house in

SPECIMEN OF THE WYANDOTT, OR HURON LANGUAGE.

One—Scat.
Two—Tin,dee.
Three—Shaight.
Four—An,daght.
Five—Wee,ish.
Six—Wa,shaw.
Seven—Soo,ta,re.
Eight—Ace,tarai.
Nine—Ain,tru.
Ten—Augh,sagh.
Twenty—ten,deit,a,waugh,sa.
Thirty—Shaigh,ka,waugh,sa.
Forty—An,dagh,ka,waugh,sa.
Fifty—Wee,ish,a,waugh,sa.
Sixty—Waw,shaw,wagh,sa.
Seventy—Soo,ta,re,waugh,sa.
Eighty—Au,tarai,waugh,sa.
Ninety—Ain,tru,waugh,sa.
One hundred—Scu,te,main,gar,we.
The great God, or good spirit—Ta,main,de,zue.
Good—Ye,waugh,ste.
Bad—Waugh,she.
Devil, or bad spirit—Deghshee,re,noh.
Heaven—Ya,roh,nia.
Hell—Degh,shunt.
Sun—Ya,an,des,hra.
Moon—Waugh,sunt,ya,an,des,hra.
Stars—Tegh,she.
Sky—Cagh,ro,ni,ate.
Clouds—Oght,se,rah.
Wind—Iru,quas.
It rains—Ina,un,du,se.
Thunder—Heno.
Lightning—Tim,mendi,quas.
Earth—Umait,sagh.
Deer—Ough,scan,oto.
Bear—Anu,e.
Raccoon—Ha,in,te,roh.
Fox—Th,na,in,ton,to.
Beaver—Soo,taie.
Mink—So,hoh,main,dia.
Turkey—Daigh,ton,tah.
Squirrel—Ogh,ta,eh.
Otter—Ta,wen,deh.
Dog—Yun,ye,nah.
Cow—Kin,ton,squa,ront.
Horse—Ugh,shut,te, or man carrier.
Goose—Yah,hounk.
Duck—Yu,in,geh.
Man—Air,ga,hon.
Woman—Utch,ke.
Girl—Ya,weet,sen,tho.
Boy—Oma,int,sent,e,hah.
Child—Che,ah,ha.
Old man—Ha,o,tong.
Old woman—Ut,sindag,sa.
My wife—Azut,tun,oh,oh.
Corn—Nay,hah.
Beans—Yah,re,sah.
Potatoes—Da,ween,dah.
Mellons, or pumpkins—O,nugh,sa.

Grass—E,ru,ta.
Weeds—Ha,en,tan.
Trees—Ye,aron,ta.
Wood—O,tagh,ta.
House—Ye,anogh,sha.
Gun—Who,ra,min,ta.
Powder—T'egh,sta.
Lead—Ye,at,ara.
Flints—Ta,wegh,ske,ra.
Knife—We,ne,ash,ra.
Axe—Otto,ya,ye.
Blanket—Deengh,tai,sea.
Kettle—Ya,yan,e,tith.
Rum—We,at,se,wie.
River—Ye,an,da,wa.
Bread—Da,ta,rah.
Dollar—Sogh,ques,tut.
Shirt—Ca,tu,reesh.
Leggins—Ya,ree.
Bell—Te,ques,ti,egh,tas,ta.
Saddle—Quagh.she,ta.
Bridle—Cong,shu,ree.
Fire—Sees,ta.
Flour—Ta,ish,rah.
Hog—Quis,quesh.
Big house—Ye,a,nogh,shu,wan,a.
Corn field—Ya,yan,quagh,ke.
Musk rat—Se,he,ash,i,ya,hah.
Cat—Dush,rat.
Wild cat—Skaink,qua,hagh.
Mole—Ca,in,dia,he,nugh,qua.
Snake—To,en,gen,seek.
Frog—Sun,day,wa,shu,ka.
Americans—Sa,ray,u,migh, or big knives.
Englishman—Qu,han,stro,no.
Frenchman—Tu,bugh,car,o,no.
My Brother—Ha,en,ye,ha.
My sister—A,en,ya,ha.
Father—Ha,yes,ta.
Mother—Ane,heh.
Sick—Shat,wu,ra.
Well—Su,we,regh,he.
Cold—Ture,a.
Warm—Ote,re,a,ute.
Snow—De,neh,ta.
Ice—Deesh,ra.
Water—Sa,un,dus,tee,the, the origin of Sandusky, the bay, river and county of that name.
Friend—Ne,at,a,rugh.
Enemy—Ne,mat,re,zue.
War—Tre,zue.
Peace—Scan,o,nie.
Are you married—Scan,dai,ye.
I am not married yet—Augh,sogh,a,sante,te,sandai,ge.
Come here—Owa,he.
Go away—Sa cati,arin,ga.
You trouble me—Ska,in,gen,tagh,qua.
I am afraid—I,agh,ka,ron,se.
I love you—Yu,now,moi,e.
I hate you—Yung,squa,his.

which the said Elizabeth Whitaker now lives.

To Robert Armstrong, who was taken prisoner by the Indians, and has ever since lived among them, and has married a Wyandot woman, one section, to contain 640 acres of land, on the west side of the Sandusky river, to begin at a place called Camp Ball, and to run up the river, with the meanders thereof, 160 poles, and from the extremity of these lines west for quantity.

To the children of the late William M'Collock, who was killed in August 1812, near Maugaugon, and who are quarter-blood Wyandot Indians, one section, to contain 640 acres of land, on the west side of the Sandusky river, adjoining the lower line of the tract hereby granted to Robert Armstrong, and extending in the same manner with and from the said river.

To John Vanmeter, who was taken prisoner by the Wyandots, and who has ever since lived among them, and has married a Seneca woman, and to his wife's three brothers, Senecas, who now reside on Honey Creek, 1000 acres of land, to begin north, 45 degrees west, 140 poles from the house in which the said John Vanmeter now lives, and to run thence, south, 320 poles, thence, and from the beginning, east for quantity.

To Sarah Williams, Joseph Williams and Rachel Nugent, later Rachel Williams, the said Sarah having been taken prisoner by the Indians, and ever since lived among the, and being the widow, and the said Joseph and Rachel being the children, of the late Isaac Williams, a half-blood Wyandot, one quarter section of land, to contain 160 acres, on the east side of the Sandusky river, below Croghansville, and to include their improvements at a place called Negro Point.

To Catherine Walker, a Wyandot woman, and to John R. Walker, her son, who was wounded in the service of the United States, at the battle of Mauguagon in 1812, a section of 640 acres of land each, to begin at the northwestern corner of the tract hereby granted to John Vanmeter and his wife's brothers, and to run with the line thereof, south, 320 poles, thence, and from the beginning, west for quantity.

To Horonu or the Cherokee Boy, a Wyandot (son of Half King) chief, a section of land, to contain 640 acres on the Sandusky river, to be laid off in square form, and to include his improvements." (INDIAN AFFAIRS: LAWS AND TREATIES, Volume II, Kappler. Washington, D.C.: 1904)

Wyandot chiefs who were instrumental in signing the preceeding treaty were: Dunquad or Half King, Runtunda or War Pole, Hronuc or Cherokee Boy, T. Aruntue or Between the Logs, D. Wottondt or John Hicks, T. Undetaso or George Punch, Menonkue or Thomas and Undauwau or Matthews.

After distribution of the fifteen sections, the remainder of the 12 miles square was divided equally among: Hoocue, Roudootouk, Mahoma, Naatoua, Mautanawto, Maurunquaws, Naynuhanky, Abraham Williams Sen., Squautaugh, Tauyouranuta, Tahawquevouws, Dasharows, Trayhetou, Hwtooyou, Maydounaytove, Neudooslau, Deecalrautousay, Houtooyemaugh, Datoowawna, Matsaye-aayourie, James Ranken, Sentumass, Tahautoshowweda, Madudara, Shaudauaye, Shamadeesay, Soomodowot, Moautaau, Nawsottomaugh, Maurawskinquaws, Tawtoolowme, Shawdouyeayourou, Showweno, Dashoree, Sennewdorow, Toayttooraw, Mawskattaugh, Tahawshodeuyea, Haunarawreudee, Shauromou, Tawyaurontoreyea, Roumelay, Nadocays, Carryumanduetaugh, Bigarms, Madonrawcays, Haurauoot, Syhrundash, Tahorowtsemdee, Roosayn, Dautoresay, Nashawtoomons, Skawduutoutee, Sanorowsha, Nautennee, YOuausha, Aumatourow, Ohoutautoon, Tawyougaustayou, Sootonteeree, Dootooau, Hawreewaucudee, Yourahatsa, Towntoreshaw, Syuwewataugh, Cauyou, Omitztseshaw, Gausawaugh, Skashowaysquaw, Mawdovdoo, Narowayshaus, Nawcatay, Isuhowhayeato, Myatousha, Tauoodowma, Youhreo, George Williams, Oharvatoy, Saharosor,

Isaac Williams, Squindatee, Mayeatohot, Lewis Coon, Isatouque or John Coon, Tawaumanocay or E. Wright, Owawtatuu, Isontraudee, Tomatsahoss, Sarrahoss, Tauyoureehoryeow, Saudotoss, Toworordu or Big Ears, Tauomatsaarau, Tahoroudoyou or Two, Daureehau, Dauoreenu, Trautohauweetough, Yourowquains or widow of the Crane, Caunaytoma, Hottomorrow, Taweesho, Dauquausay, Toumou, Hoogaudoorow, Newdeetoutow, Dawhowhouk, Daushouteehawk, Sawaronuis, Norrorow, Tawwass, Tawareroons, Neshaustay, Toharratough, Taurowtotucawaa, Youshindauyato, Tauosanays, Sadowerrais, Isanowtowtouk or Fox Widow, Sauratoudo or William Zane, Hayanoise or Ebenezer Zane, Mawcasharrow or widow M'Cullock, Susannah, Teshawtaugh, Dawews, Tamataurank, Razor, Rahisaus, Cudeetore, Shawnetaurew,

Tatrarow, Cuqua, Yourowon, Sauyounaoskra, Tanorawayout, Howcuquawdorow, Gooyeamee, Dautsaqua, Maudamu, Sanoreeshoc, Hauleeyeatausay, Gearoohee, Matokrawtouk, Dawweeshoe, Sawyourawot, Nacudseoranauaurayk, Youronurays, Scoutash, Serroymuch, Hoondeshotch, Ishuskeah, Dusharraw, Ondewaus, Duyewtale, Roueyoutacolo, Hoonorowyoutacob, Hownorowduro, Nawanaunonelo, Tolhomanona, Chiyamik, Tyyeakwheunohale, Aushewhowole, Schowondashres, Mondushawquaw, Tayoudrakele, Giveriahes, Sootreeshuskoh, Suyouturaw, Tiudee, Tahorroshoquaw, Irahkasquaw, Ishoreameusuwat,

Curoweyottell, Noriyettete, Siyarech and Testeatete.

Another treaty dated in 1818 was given to the Wyandots on the Sandusky. Signing that treaty for them were: Douquad or Half King, Rontondu or War Pole, Tuayaurontoyou or Between the Logs, Dauatout or John Hicks, Horonu or Cherokee Boy, Teoudetoss or George Punch, Hawdoro or Matthews, Skoutous and Quouqua.

On January 19, 1832, the Wyandots in Crawford County, Ohio gave up their land to move to Canada or river Huron in Michigan or where they owned a reservation of land.

Signing that treaty for that group of Wyandots were: Roenunas, Bearskin, Shiawa or John Solomon, John McLean, Matthew Grey Eyes, Isaac Driver, John D. Brown and Alex. Clarke.

Finally in March 1842 the Wyandots were removed to a reservation west of the Mississippi River or west of the Missouri River. Those individuals who received a section of land each were: Silas Armstrong, John M. Armstrong, Matthew R. Walker, William Walker, Joel Walker, Charles B. Garrett, George Garrett, George J. Clark, Irwin P. Long, Ethan A. Long, Joseph L. Tennery, Robert Robertaile, Jared S. Dawson, Joseph Newell, John T. Walker, Peter D. Clark, James Rankin, Samuel McCulloch, Elliot McCulloch, Isaiah Walker, William M. Tennery, Henry Clay Walker, Ebenezer Z. Reed amd Joel Walker Garrett.

The following chiefs and councillors likewise received a section of land each: Francis A. Hicks, James Washington, Squeendehtee, Henry Jaques, Tauroonee, Doctor Grey Eyes, George Armstrong, Warpole, John Hicks, Peacock and George Punch.

Thus after 1842, the Wyandots were no longer in the state of Ohio.

THE SHAWNEES
CHAPTER FIVE

August 3, 1795 Treaty with the Shawnees, Wyandots, Delawares, Ottawas, Chippewas, Potawatomis, Miamis, Eel-River, Weas, Kickapoos, Piankashaws, Kaskaskias. Greenville meeting to establish new boundaries in Ohio. Earlier treaties deemed null and void.

July 4, 1805 Treaty with the Shawnees, Wyandots, Chippewas, Munsee, Delawares, and Potawatomi held at Fort Industry, Ohio. A new boundary line established between tribal lands and United States.

November 25, 1808 Treaty with the Shawnees, Chippewas, Ottawas, Potawatomis, and Wyandots at Brownstown, Michigan. Boundaries for those residing in Michigan and Ohio redrawn.

September 29, 1817 Treaty with the Shawnees, Wyandots, Senecas, Delwares, Potawatomis, Ottawas and Chippewas concluded at Rapids of the Miami in Ohio. Smaller tracts of Ohio land granted to tribes and certain individuals.

September 18, 1818 Treaty with the Shawnees, Wyandots, Senecas, Ottawas, Delawares, Potawatomis and Chippewas at St. Mary's, Ohio. Grants given in 1817 to be considered only as reservations for the use of the tribes. Additional tracts granted to the Shawnees, Wyandots and Senecas.

July 20, 1831 Treaty with the Shawnees, Wyandots and Senecas at Lewistown, Ohio. Tribes around Lewistown willing to move west of Mississippi River.

August 8, 1831 Treaty with the Shawnees at Wapaghkonnetta, Allen County, Ohio. Tribes ceding land to United States for that west of the Mississippi River.

The early history of the Chaouanons (Shawano, changed to Shawanoes, Shawanee and ultimately to Shawnee) belongs to the great Algonquin family of the St. Lawrence country. The home of this division of the tribe, within the historic period, was the valley of the Cumberland. Here they lived until the Iroquois took the war path in 1655 when they were called upon to defend their hunting grounds.

From this time to 1672 a relentless war was waged which resulted in their defeat and expulsion. They fled southward, some locating in the Carolinas, others at the head of the Mobile River in Florida, while others wandered into New Spain. After a few years, however, the remnants of the tribe were collected, and all joined in the enterprise of repossessing their ancient hunting grounds.

In 1682 a peace was concluded between the Iroquois and Shawnees, and the same year the former entrusted the latter tribe with the care of the Treaty-parchment on which their agreement with William Penn was recorded.

The treaty between William Penn and the Indians made in 1682 was the first treaty with the Americans in which the Shawnees participated. From that time up to 1832 the Quakers took a lively interest in this tribe.

In 1701 the conference between Wapatha, representing the Indians, and Penn, representing the Americans, was held at Philadelphia. No treaty was under consideration as it was rather a friendly meeting in which each pledged his party to carry out the principles of peace and friendship.

In 1715 the Chief Opessah represented this tribe at Philadelphia in the inter-tribal council, and he was undoubtedly, the first chief of the Shawnees inhabiting northwestern Ohio, where, by this time, they pretended to have title to some of the Wyandot and Miami hunting grounds.

The depredations of the Shawnees upon the settlements in Virginia caused Gov. Dunmore in 1774 to send an army for the invasion of the Indian tribes on the Scioto and Little Miami in Ohio.

In September 1774 a great battle was fought at the junction of the Great Kanawha with the Ohio, in which the Shawnees and their allies were defeated and compelled to beat a hasty retreat across the Ohio River. The Shawnees were led by Cornstalk, a great chief, aided by the celebrated chief and warrior Blackhoof. In the fall of 1774 Gov. Dunmore held a treaty in which Cornstalk, Blackhoof, Logan, the Grenadier Squaw and other noted Indians participated. Peace was proclaimed but was of short duration because of the onslaught of settlers on the frontier.

In 1777 Cornstalk, another chief Red Hawk and Cornstalk's son Ellinipsico were murdered in retaliation by angry settlers which created instability until the peace of 1795 signed at Greenville. Those Shawnees present at the treaty of Greenville were: Blue Jacket, Red Pole, Pucksekaw, Black Wolf, Lame Hawk, Blackhoof, Keeahah, Kekiapilathy and Captain Johnny.

After the treaty, in the years 1807 to 1810 the Shawnees began to fall back on their reserves. Prior to the treaty of 1795 they were scattered much all over Ohio and along the streams in Indiana.

While residing on the Mad River, the Shawnees were divided into four tribes: the Piqua, Kiskapocke, Mequachuke and Chillicothe. According to a poetical Indian legend, the Piqua tribe had its origin in a man who sprang from the fire and ashes. As their old men used to tell the settlers who first came in contact with them, the chief warriors and wise men were once sitting around the smoldering embers of what had been a council fire, when they were startled by a great puffing of fire and smoke, and from the ashes and coals, there sprang into being a man of splendid form and mein, the original of the tribe of Piqua -- named Piqua as signifying the man born of ashes.

Mequachuke signifies a fat man filled -- a man made perfect, so that nothing is wanting. This tribe had the priesthood. Its leaders were endowed with the priviledge of celebrating the religious rites of the nation.

The Kiskapocke tribe were the most aggressive tribes of the Northwest. The celebrated prophet, and Tecumseh, his brother, were members of this tribe.

Chillicothe is not known to have been interpreted save as meaning a dwelling place. The Shawnees were the only tribe among the Indians of the Northwest who had a tradition of foreign origin and held a yearly festival to celebrate the safe arrival in this country of their ancestors.

Their towns were scattered along the banks of the Scioto, the Mad River, and the Little Miami, in southern

VOCABULARY OF THE SHAWANOESE.

One—Negate.
Two—Neshwa.
Three—Nithese.
Four—Newe.
Five—Nialinwe.
Six—Negotewathe.
Seven—Neshwathe.
Eight—Sashekswa.
Nine—Chakatswa.
Ten—Metathwe.
Eleven—Metath,we, Kit,en,e,gate.
Twelve—Metathwe, Kiteneshwa.
Thirteen—Metathwe, Kitenithwa.
Fourteen—Metathwe, Kitenewa.
Fifteen—Metathwe, Kitenealinwe.
Sixteen—Metathwe, Kitenegotewathe.
Seventeen—Metathwe, Kiteneshwathe.
Eighteen—Metathwe, Kitensashekswa.
Nineteen—Metathwe, Kitenchakatswe.
Twenty—Neesh,wa,tee,tuck,e.
Thirty—Nithwabetucke.
Forty—Newabetucke.
Fifty—Nialinwabetucke.
Sixty—Negotewashe.
Seventy—Neshwashe.
Eighty—Swashe.
Ninety—Chaka.
One hundred—Te,pa,wa.
Two hundred—Neshwatepawa.
Three hundred—Nithwatepawa.
Four hundred—Newe-tepawa.
Five hundred—Nialinwe-tepawa.
Six hundred—Negotewathe-tepawa.
Seven hundred—Neshwethe-tepawa.
Eight hundred—Sashekswa-tepawa.
Nine hundred—Chakatswe-tepawa.
One thousand—Metathwe-tepawa.
Two thousand—Neshina,metathwe,tepawa.
Three thousand—Nethina,metathwe,tepawa.
Four thousand—Newena,metathwe tepawa.
Five thousand—Nealinwa metathwe tepawa.
Old man—Pasnetome.
Young man—Meanesenex.

Chief—Okema.
Dog—Weshe.
Horse—Meshewa.
Cow—Methothe.
Sheep—Meketha.
Hog—Kosko.
Cat—Posetha.
Turkey—Pelewa.
Deer—Peshikthe.
Raccoon—Ethepate.
Bear—Mugwa.
Otter—Kitate.
Mink—Chaquiwashe.
Wild cat—Peshewa.
Panther—Meshepeshe.
Buffalo—Methoto.
Elk—Wabete.
Fox—Wawakotchethe.
Musk rat—Oshasqua.
Beaver—Amaghqua.
Swan—Wabethe.
Goose—Neeake.
Duck—Sheshepuk.
Fish—Amatha.
Tobacco—Siamo.
Canoe—Olagashe.
Big vessel or ship—Misheologashe.
Paddle—Shumaghtee.
Saddle—Appapewee.
Bridle—Shaketonebetchexa.
Man—Elene.
Woman—Equiwa.
Boy—Skillewaythetha.
Girl—Squithetha.
Child—Apetotha.
My wife—Neewa.
Your wife—Keewa.
My husband—Wysheana.
Your husband—Washetohe.
My father—Notha.
Your father—Kotha.
My mother—Neegah.
Grandmother—Cocumtna.

NAMES OF RIVERS BY THE SHAWANOESE—SPOKEN SHA,WA,NO.

Ohio, i. e. Eagle river.—See page 574.
Ken,a,wa—meaning having whirlpools, or swallowing up. Some have it that an evil spirit lived in the water, which drew substances to the bottom of the river.
Sci,o,to was named by the Wyandotts, who formerly resided upon it. A large town was at Columbus, having their cornfields on the bottom grounds opposite that city. The Wyandotts pronounce the word *Sci,on,to*, signification unknown.
Great Miamie—Shi,me,a,mee,sepe, or Big Miamie.
Little Miamie—Che,ke,me,a,mee,sepe, or Little Miamie.
Mus,king,um is a Delaware word, and means a town on the river side. The Shawanoes call it Wa,ka,ta,mo,sepe, which has the same signification.
Hock,hock,ing is Delaware, and means a bottle. The Shawanoese have it Wea,tha,kagh,qua,sepe—Bottle river.
Augl ze river—Cow,the,na,ke,sepe, or falling timber river.
Saint Mary's river—Ca,ko,the,ke,sepe, or kettle river—cako,the,ke, a kettle.
Miamie of the lake—Ot,ta,wa,sepe, or Ottawa river. The Ottawas had several towns on this river as late as 1811, and down to within 10 years. They occupied the country about the lake shore, Maumee bay and the rapids above Perrysburgh.
Blanchard's fork of the Auglaize—Sha,po,qua,te, sepe, or Tailor's river. See p. 237.
Sandusky river—called by the Shawanoese Po,ta,ke,sepe, a rapid river.
Detroit strait, or river—Ke,ca,me,ge, the narrow passage, or strait.
Kentucky is a Shawanoese word, and signifies at the head of a river.
Licking river, which enters the Ohio opposite the city of Cincinnati—the Shawanoese have it, Ne,pe,pim,me,sepe, from Ne,pe,pim,me, salt, and sepe, river, i. e. salt river.
Mad river—by the Shawanoese, Athe,ne,sepe,athe,ne, a flat or smooth stone, and sepe, river, i. e. a flat or smooth stone river.

Ohio. Cornstalk, the great chief, so cruelly assassinated at Point Pleasant, resided east of the Scioto River, on Sippo Creek, in what is now Pickaway County, and his sister, the Grenadier Squaw, who was six feet high, resided near him on the opposite side of the stream, in Squaw Town.

The principal town, Old Chillicothe, was located near the mouth of Massie's Creek, three miles north of the present site of Xenia. Piqua, memorable as the birthplace of Tecumseh and Elsquatawa, was situated on the north bank of Mad River, seven miles west of the present site of the city of Springfield, in Clark County. Upper and Lower Piqua, in Miami County, were not far from the present site of the city of Piqua.

When the troops under Gen. Logan destroyed the Mequachake towns on Mad River in 1786, the Shawnees fled toward the wilderness at the head of the Auglaize and Ottawa Rivers, where game abounded, and where they would have time and protection to concoct their plans.

In the treaty signed at Greenville in August 1795, several Shawnee affixed their signatures: Misquacoonacaw or Red Pole, Cutthewekasaw or Black Hoof, Kaysewaesekah, Weythapamattha, Nianymseka, Waytheah or Long Shanks, Weyapiersenwaw or Blue Jacket, Nequetanghaw, Hahgooseekaw or Captain Reed.

Another treaty was made in July 1805 where the Shawnees and others made cessions to the United States. Chiefs signing for the Shawnees were: Weyapurseawaw or Blue Jacket, Cutheaweasaw or Blackhoof, Auonasechla or Civil Man and Isaac Peters.

Three years later at Brownstown, Michigan, further boundaries were established for the Indian territories. Black Hoof or Makatewekasha and Koitawaypie or Col. Lewis were the Shawnees representing their tribe.

In the fall of 1811 a good deal of uneasiness existed among the Shawnees, Delawares, Wyandots and other western tribes, and British agents were very active in their endeavors to seduce the Ohio Indians into the British service, in case of a war with the United States.

By a treaty held at Maumee Rapids in 1817 by Gen. Lewis Cass and Duncan McArthur, the Shawnees were given a reservation around Wapakonetta, in the name of Blackhoof, and along Hog Creek, of ten miles square. Chiefs at Wapakonetta receiving tracts within that area were: Catewekesa or Black Hoof, Byaseka or Wolf, Pomthe or Walker, Shemenetoo or Big Snake, Othawakeseka or Yellow Feather, Chakalowah or the Tail's End, Pemthala or John Perry, and

Wabepee or White Colour. Tracts were also given to the Shawnee chiefs on Hog Creek: Peeththa or Falling Tree and Onowaskemo or Resolute Man. The Lewistown chiefs receiving tracts were: Quatawape or Captain John Lewis said to have married Mary, the Indian sister of the captive Jonathan Alder, Shekaghkela or Turtle and Skilowa or Robin.

Other special land grants were given to: Nancy Stewart, daughter of the late Shawnee chief Blue Jacket, who received 640 acres on the Great Miami River below Lewistown; and to the children of the late Shawnee chief Captain Logan or Spamagelabe, 640 acres on the east side of the Auglaize River adjoining the ten mile tract at Wapaghkonetta.

Again the remaining parcels were equally divided among those at Wapakonetta, mostly within the present bounds of Allen County: Blackhoof, Pamthee or Walker, Peaseca or Wolf, Shemanita or Snake, Athelwakesoca or Yellow Clouds, Pemthewtew or John Perry, Cacalawa or End of the Tail, Quelawe, War Chief, Sacachewa, Werewela, Wasawotah or Bright Horn, Otharasa or Yellow, Tepeteseca, Newahetucca, Caawaricho, Thacatchewa, Silochaheca, Tapea or Sanders, Mesherawah, Toleapea, Pochecaw, Alawemetahuck or Lullaway or Perry,

Wawelame, Nemecashe, Nerupeneshequal or Cornstalk, Shicho, Shealawhe, Naskaka, Thacaska or David McNair, Shapukaha, Quacowawnee, Necoshecu, Thucusen or Jim Blue Jacket, Chowelaseca, Quahaho, Kayketchheka or William Perry, Sewapen, Peetah or Davy Baker, Skapoawah or George McDongal, Chepocura, Shoma or Sam, Cheahaska or Capt. Tommy, Gen. Wayne, Theway, Ohawee, Wearecah,

Capt. Reed, Lawaytucheh or John Wolf, Tecutio or Gurge, Skekacumpskekaw, Wishemaw, Mugwaymanotreka, Quaskee, Thoswa, Baptista, Maywealiupe, Pereacumme, Chochkelake or Dam, Kewapea, Egatacumshequa, Walupe, Aquashequa, Pemata, Nepaho, Tapesheka, Lathowaynoma, Sawacotu or Yellow Clouds, Memhisheka, Ashelukah, Ohipwah, Thapaeca, Chucatuh, Nekakeka,

Thithueculu, Pelaculbe, Pelaske, Shesholou, Quanako, Halkootu, Laughshena, Capawah, Ethewacase, Quahethu, Capia, Thucatrouwah or the Going up the Hill, Magathu, Tecumtequa, Tetecopatha, Kekusthe, Sheatwah, Shealewarron, Haghkela, Akapee or Heap up Anything, Lamotothe, Kaska, Panhoar, Penitchthamtah or Peter Cornstalk, Capes, Shuagunme, Wawlepesshecco, Calequa,

Tetotu, Tashishec, Nawebesheco or White Feather, Sheperkiscoshe, Nartekah, Shemakib, Pesheto, Theatsheta, Milhametche, Chacod, Lawathska, Pachetah, Awaybariskecaw,

Hatocuino, Thomasheshawkah, Pepacoshe, Oahashe, Quelaoshu, Mewithaquiu, Ageupeh, and Quellime, these being all the males living at that time.

Those residing at Hog Creek Reservation, many of whom resided at the village where the council-house was built, afterward the farm in the 1830's for Ezekiel Hover, were: Peaithchtha, Oreroimo or Little Fox, Onawaskine, Pamathawwah or George Williams, Wapeskekahothew, Pahaweou, Shinagawmashe, Nequakabuchka, Peliska, Ketuchepa, Lawetcheto, Epaunnee, Kanakhib, Joso or Joseph Parks, Lawnoetuchu or Billy Parks, Shawnaha, Waymatalhaway, Ketoawsa, Sheshecopea, Lecuseh, Quilna, and Quedaska. Again this was the male population.

At Lewistown in 1831, special provisions were made for James McPherson and Henry H. McPherson, and Martin Lane, an interpreter who had married a part Seneca woman. At Wapaghkonnetta in 1831, Joseph Parks, an interpreter who was a quarter Shawnee received special provision.

As the time for removal of the tribe to Kansas came nearer and nearer in 1832, the Shawnees were observed to grow more dull and listless. With the arrival of David Robb and D. M. Workman among them, they realized truly that they must leave their old hunting grounds forever, and with this realization, each lodge entered on a special method of making the occasion memorable.

Many surrendered themselves to despair, and plunged into a course of dissipation; others, with more regard to the legends of the tribe, collected their trophies, articles of chase, domestic utensils, andn even leveled the mounds of the burial grounds of the tribe.

This accomplished, the sub-agents Robb and Workman gave the order to proceed on that long western journey, and 700 members of the Shawnee family, with half that number of Senecas, moved toward the west in September 1832, and traveled until Christmas of that year, when they camped on their Kansas reservation. Joseph Parks conducted them from the Mississippi westward. John McIlvaine and James B. Gardner accompanied them to the Mississippi. In 1833 fifty left for Kansas. A large number of Indians visited among other tribes until 1833 and 1834, revisited their old home on the Auglaize and next followed the western trail.

THE SENECAS
CHAPTER SIX

September 29, 1817 Treaty with the Senecas, Delawares, Wyandots, Shawnees, Potawatomis, Ottawas and Chippewas at Rapids of the Miami, Ohio. Smaller tracts granted to tribes and certain individuals.

September 18, 1818 Treaty with the Senecas, Wyandots, Shawnees, Ottawas, Delawares, Potawatomis and Chippewas at St. Mary's, Ohio. Grants given in 1817 to be considered only as reservations for the use of the tribes. Additional tracts granted to the Senecas, Shawnees and Wyandots.

February 28, 1831 Treaty with the Senecas on the Sandusky River, Ohio at Washington, D.C. Tribe agreed to move to west of the Mississippi.

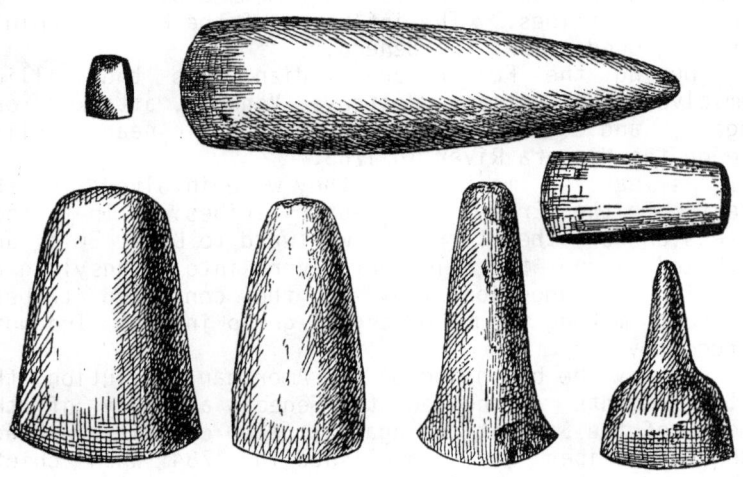

WEDGE-SHAPED IMPLEMENTS.

The Senecas were a branch of the Iroquois confederacy, and called themselves by a name meaning "people of the mountain." When first known to settlers or colonists, they occupied lands in western New York between Seneca Lake and Genesee River.

From the Jesuit Relation for 1635, the Seneca after defeating the Hurons or Wyandots in the spring of 1634 made peace with them. The Hurons in the following year sent an embassy to Sonontouan, the chief town of the Seneca to ratify the peace, and while there learned that the Onondaga, the Oneida, the Cayuga and the Mohawk were wanting to join the treaty.

In 1639 the war was renewed by the Hurons who in May had captured 12 prisoners from the Seneca. By 1643 a band of 300 Seneca attacked the village of the Aondironnons which began the war between the Iroquois and the Neuters.

The Seneca continued the aggression through 1649 and finally defeated the Neuters and the Eries. They joined forces with the Mohawk in 1652 to destroy the French settlements on the St. Lawrence. Difficult relations existed between the Seneca and French until 1655 when the French attempted to establish Jesuit missions among the Seneca.

By 1657 the Seneca in imitating the Iroquois League by absorbing conquered tribes had a membership composed of 11 different tribes. The influence of the French rapidly gained ground among the Seneca.

During the French and Indian wars they allied themselves with Pontiac, destroyed Venango, attacked Fort Niagara, and cut off a British supply train near Devil's Hole on the Niagara River in 1763.

As earlier mentioned, they were involved in the defeat of the Eries and Neuter tribes. They took possession of the territory westward to Lake Erie and southward along the Allegheny River into Pennsylvania, receiving by adoption many of the conquered tribes, therefore making them the largest group in the Iroquois confederacy.

But by the beginning of the American Revolution, the British agents reconciled the Senecas and many of the others of the Six Nations against the colonies. Peace with the tribes was accomplished in 1784 when chiefs Tayagonendagighti and Tehonwaeghrigagi represented their tribes in establishing boundaries.

A group of Seneca split from the major in New York sometime before 1792 and moved west to the Sandusky River in Ohio, near where the city of Sandusky now is.

Conjecture has raised the question of whether the Seneca at Sandusky were really Seneca. They were called Seneca but many feel that the group was largely subjugated Erie and Conestoga. Others have indicated that the group was a remnant of Logan's tribe, as Logan was Conestoga or Mingo on his maternal side.

The Sandusky Senecas were involved in the treaty in 1817 when other tribes in the area also made cessions. Chiefs Tahawmadoyaw, Captain Harris, Isahownusay, Joseph Tawgyou, Captain Smith, CoffeeHouse, Running About and Wiping Stick represented their tribes in this transaction on the Sandusky River. Lewistown Seneca chiefs were: Mesomea or Civil John, Wakawuxsheno or the White Man, Oquasheno or Joe, and Willaquasheno or When You Are Tired Sit Down. William Spicer, who was taken prisoner by the Indians and has ever since lived among them, and had married a Seneca woman, received a section of land on the bank of the Sandusky River.

Affixing their marks to that treaty were chiefs: Methomea or Civil John, Sacoureweeghta or Whiping Stick, Shekoghkell or Big Turtle, Aquasheno or Joe, Wakenuceno or White Man, Samendue or Captain Sigore, Skilleway or Robbin, and Dasquoerunt.

Other Senecas receiving equal parcels in the thirty thousand acres were:

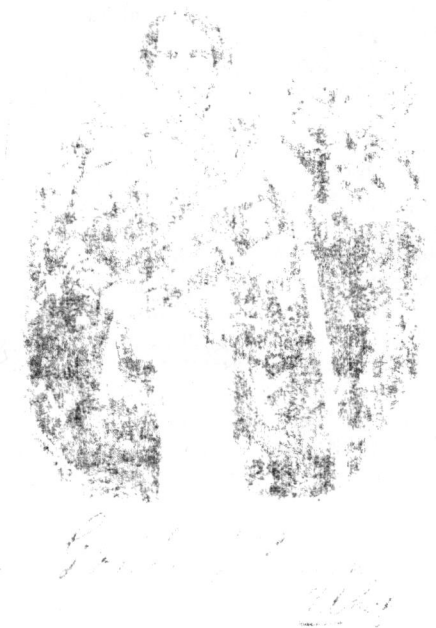

Syuwasautau, Nawwene, Joseph, Iseumetaugh or Picking Up a Club, Orawhaotodie or Turn Over, Saudaurous or Split the River, Tahowtoorains or Jo Smee, Ispomduare Yellowbay, Dashowrowramou or Drifting Sand, Hauautounasquas, Hamyautuhow, Tahocayn, Howdautauyeao or King George,

Standing Bones, Cyahaga or Fisher, Suthemoore, Red Skin, Mentauteeboore, Hyanashraman or Knife in His Hand, Running About, John Smith, Carrying the Basket, Cauwauay or Striking, Rewauyeato or Carrying the News, Half Up the Hill, Trowyoudoys or G. Hunter,

Spike Buck, Caugooshow or Clearing Up, Mark on His Hip, Captain Hams, Isetaune or Crying Often, Taunerowyea or Two Companies, Haudonwauays or Stripping the River, Isohauhasay or Tall Chief, Tahowmandoyou, Howyouway or Paddling, Clouding Up, Youwautowtoyou or Burnt His Body, Shetouyouwee or Sweet Foot,

Tauhaugainstoany or Holding His Hand About, Oharrawtodee or Turning Over, Haucaumarout, Sarrowsauismatare or Striking Sword, Sadudeto, Oshoutoy or Burning Berry, Hard Hickery, Curetscetau, Youronocay or Isaac, Youtradowwonlee, Newtauyaro, Tayouonte or Old Foot, Tauosanetee, Syunout or Give It to Her, Doonstough or Hunch on His Forehead, Tyaudusout or Joshua Hendricks, Taushaushaurow or Cross the Arms, Henry, Youwaydauyea or the Island,

Armstrong, Shake the Ground, His Neck Down, Youheno, Towotoyoudo or Looking at Her, Captain Smith, Tobacco, Standing Stone, Ronunaise or Wiping Stick, Tarsduhatse or Large Bones, Hamanchagave, House Fly or Maggot, Roudouma or Sap Running, Big Belt, Cat Bone, Sammy, Taongauats or Round the Point,

Ramuye or Hold the Sky, Mentoududu, Hownotant, Slippery Nose, Tauslowquowsay or Twenty Wives, Hoogaurow or Mad Man, Coffee House and Long Hair.

Senecas receiving parcels at Lewistown were: Civil John, Wild Duck, Tall Man, Molasses, Ash, Nahanexa, Tasauk, Agusquenah, Roughleg, Quequesaw, Playful, Hairlip, Sieutinque, Hillnepewayatuska, Tauhunsequa, Nynoah, Suchusque, Leemutque, Treuse, Sequate, Caumecus, Scowneti, Tocondusque, Conhowdatwaw, Cowista, Nequatren, Cowhousted, Gillwas, Axtaca, Conawwehow, Sutteasee, Kiahoot, Crane, Silver, Bysaw, Crayfiste, Woolyhead, Conundahaw, Shacosaw, Coindos, Hutchequa, Nayau, Connodose, Coneseta, Neslauuta, Owl, Couauka, Cocheco, Couewash, Sinnecowacheckowe or Leek.

Another treaty in 1818 again establishing boundaries in Ohio was signed by the Senecas and other tribes. Signing their marks for the tribes were: Methomea or Civil John,

Skekoghkell or Big Turtle, Waghkonoxie or White Bone, Tochequia or Yellow Bone, Captain Tongue, Cuueshohant or Harris, Tousonecta or His Blanket Down and Wiping Stick.

The Senecas residing on the Sandusky relinguished all their claim to Ohio lands and accepted removal to west of the Mississippi on February 28, 1831 in a treaty signed at Washington, D.C. Signing for the tribe were Coonstick, Small Cloud Spicer, Seneca Steel, Hard Hickory and Capt. Good Hunter.

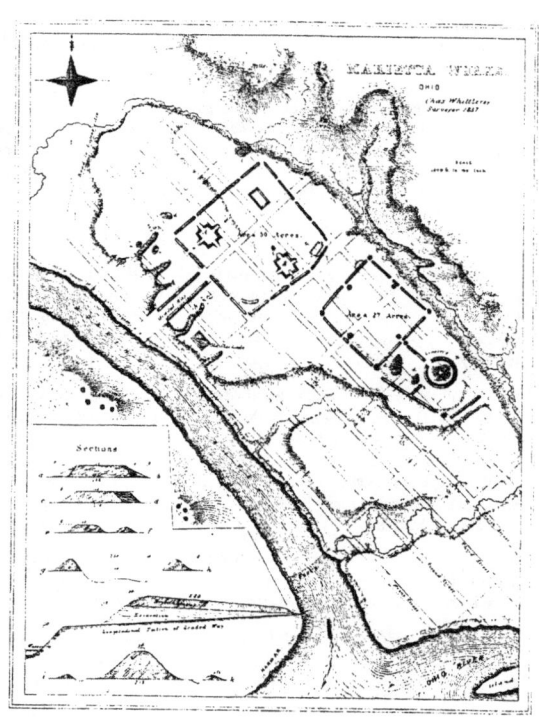

Marietta, Ohio, portrayed in an 1847 study (above and right), *grew up around a microcosm of Indian history: a grave mound of the Adena era (500 to 1 B.C.), earthen walls of Hopewell design (A.D. 1 to 300), and platform mounds, perhaps Mississippian (A.D. 800 to 1500). In 1788 Marietta designated the key sites as public squares, and citizens raised funds in 1830 to maintain them. Despite later development, some mounds survived in the 1980s.*

THE INDIAN TRIBES IN OHIO IN 1830

"There are five Indian tribes resident within the State of Ohio - the Wyandots, Senecas, Delawares, Shawnees and Ottawas. The Senecas, are composed of Cayugas 157, Mohawks 46, Oneidas 48, Onondagas 7, and Senecas 262; total 520. The Delaware tribe, however, sold out their lands, consisting of 5,760 acres in 1829.

The tradition of these tribes, claim nativity in the surrounding states and territories; and have resided in this state from fifty to two hundred years. The tradition of each tribe, preserves the name of the country from which they originally emigrated to this state. The number of persons in each tribe, have not increased for some years past. The population of each tribe, and the number of acres claimed by each, may be stated as follows:

Tribes	No.	Acres	Tribes	No.	Acres	Tribes	No.	Acres
Wyandotts	527	163,000	Senecas	520	117,000	Ottawas	377	50,581
Shawnees	500	117,000	Delawares	76	5,760			

The land claimed by each tribe is secured to them, respectively by treaty. Besides the land already stated, reservations to the amount of 16,200 are secured separately to individuals; thus making the whole amount of land secured to individuals in this state 409,401 acres. Considerable annuities are paid yearly by the national government to these tribes."

ANTIQUITIES

"The most prominent antiquities are the numerous mounds and forts of earth, in the state of Ohio. It is not known the time when, by what people, and even for what purpose, these stupendous monuments of human labor and ingenuity, were erected. Their origin is so deeply involved in the obscurity of remote antiquity.

Some of the most remarkable forts and mounds in this state, are at Worthington, at Granville, in Athens, in Marietta, in Gallipolis, in Chillicothe, on Paintcreek, 18 miles northwest from Chillicothe, on a plain three miles northeast of Chillicothe, and at Circleville, on the east bank of the Scioto river, about 60 miles in a direct line from its mouth, and on the little Miami river. There are both mounds and forts at Granville, Circleville, near Chillicothe, on Paintcreek and the little Miami.

Many of these mounds are composed of earth of a different quality from that which is found in their immediate vicinity. This seems to indicate that the earth of which they were composed was transported from some distance.

One of the most remarkable collections of these fortifications is at Circleville. The town plat includes the area of a square fort adjoining the circular one, on the east, from which the town derives its name."

From "THE OHIO GAZETTEER" pblg. 1831

PETER PORK --- AN INDIAN

Bellefontaine, Oh. May 25th, 1832.
To Duncan McArthur, Governor of Ohio

Dear Sir:
The chiefs and leading men of the Senaca and Shawanee Nations of Indians at Lewis Town have been very Importunate with me to get me to intercede with you in behalf of one of their band now confined in the Penitentiary of Ohio by the name of PETER PORK (I think). It is said he stabed a man at Fort Ball in a fit of intoxication some two years ago. These poor creatures are now about to leave the land of their Fathers forever and go far to the west; they are extremely anxious to have all their band along therefore they urge this petition in behalf of the convict promising that if you will pardon him they will immediately take him where he will never more disturb the Society of the whites. And they also say they do not wish him let out untill immediately before they start on their journey. From all I can learn in relation to the crime, the apparant penitency of the Indian, the proportion of time he has served etc...since they are going to leave the country my opinion is that if you can conceive it to be concistant with your official duty and the interest of the people of the state as well as the magesty of our laws it would be well to let him out on the account of his own happyness as well as that of his tribe in general, and I think it would effect upon the minds of the Indians towards the Whites generally That every purpose would be answered as to them if he were now pardoned that could be provided he were to serve out his other year. I hope your Excellency will find it consort and with your sence of duty to comply with the request of the unfortunate race of our fellow mortals and if so I will be much gratified. Pleas drop me a line soon and let me know so that I can inform them the result of your coveturion as they will be very anxious to hear. Yours respectfully, DAVID ROBB, Sub Indian Agent.
(Governor's Pardon Papers, State Archives of Ohio)

THE DELAWARES
CHAPTER SEVEN

January 21, 1785 Treaty with the Delawares, Wyandots, Chippewas and Ottawas concluded at Fort McIntosh. Established the boundaries between the Indian lands in Ohio.

August 3, 1795 Treaty with the Delawares, Wyandots, Shawnees, Ottawas, Chippewas, Potawatomis, Miamis, Eel-River, Weas, Kickapoos, Piankashaws and Kaskaskias made at Greenville, Ohio. Boundaries clarified between the various tribes and that of the United States.

July 4, 1805 Treaty with the Delawares, Wyandots, Ottawas, Chippewas, Munsee, Shawnees and Potawatomis made at Fort Industry on the Miami. Tribes relinquished some of their claims and tracts made smaller.

September 29, 1817 Treaty with the Delawares, Wyandots, Senecas, Shawnees, Potawatomis, Ottawas and Chippewas at the Rapids of the Miami, Ohio. Some of the tribes relinguished more land to the United States.

September 17, 1818 Treaty with the Delawares, Wyandots, Senecas, Shawnee, Ottawas, Potawatomis and Chippewas at St. Mary's, Ohio. Tracts were strictly for use of Indian reservations. Additional annuities granted.

August 3, 1829 and September 24, 1829. Treaty with the Delawares at St. Mary's, Ohio. Relinguished their tract in Ohio for land west of the Mississippi.

The Delaware are a tribe of the Algonquin family, and when first known to the colonists were dwelling in detached bands under separate sachems on the Delaware River. They styled themselves Renappi, or as now written, Lenape or Lenni Lenape, signifying "real men." The early traditional history of the Lenape is contained in their national legend, the Walam Olum.

The Dutch began trading with them in 1616, and enjoyed friendly discourse with them until 1632 when the settlement at Swanendael was utterly destroyed by a sudden attack, but trade was soon afterward resumed.

The Swedes made attempts to Christianize them and had Luther's catechism printed in their language. The Delwares claim to have come from the West with Minguas who soon afterward reduced them to the state of vassalage, and when they were conquered by the Five Nations, they were termed women by the latter.

The Delawares formed three families or clans -- the Turtle, the Turkey and the Wolf. At the time of the 1682 "walking treaty" made by William Penn, the Delawares complained that they had been defrauded in the interpretation of the treaty, and showed a reluctance to "walk," upon which the authorities called upon the Six Nations, who ordered the Delawares, as women, to retire.

The Delawares were now thrown among warring people, and, though previously mild and peaceable, they now became defensive in trying to retain their lands.

In 1751, by invitation of the Wyandots or Hurons, they began to form settlements in east Ohio, and in a few years the greater part of the Delawares were fixed upon the Muskingum and other streams in east Ohio, together with the Munsee and Mahican, who had accompanied them from the east, being driven out by the same pressure and afterward consolidating with them.

The Delawares, being now within reach of the French and backed by the western Iroquois, and in the subsequent wars up to the treaty of Greenville in 1795 showed themselves the most determined opponents of the advancing Americans.

When Colonel Boquet made his observations the Mahoning Valley was mainly occupied by the Delawares. The densest population of this Indian nation was upon the upper Muskingum and the Tuscarawas. They were numerous and held possession of the greater part of eastern Ohio.

Because of their close association with other tribes, it makes it difficult to ascertan the number at any given period after they left the Atlantic coast.

The Chippewas dwelt north of them on the lake shore, and the Mingoes, an off-shoot of the Six Nations, had several villages on the Muskingum, below the present site of Steubenville. With these exceptions the country between the Beaver and Muskingum was inhabited by people of distinctively Delaware stock. The Massasaugas, a roving tribe of hunters, were most numerous on the Mahoning. They were among the last of the Delaware nation to leave the eastern part of the present territory of Ohio.

The Delaware had been living in the Ohio country not more than a score of years, but were a more numerous and flourishing tribe than they had ever been before. Their warriors numbered not less than six hundred, but were considered inferior in strength and courage to the Wyandots, whom they called "uncles" thus acknowledging inferiority.

The Delawares accepted Christianity more readily than any other tribe. Most of their towns were in the vicinity of the forks of the Muskingum and near the mouth of the Tuscarawas. That region was the place of their tribal councils and great feasts, and is rich in Indian traditions which are called to mind by the old Indian names occurring in the local geography.

By the treaty of 1785 the Delawares occupied the soil between the rivers Cuyahoga and Miami. At this time there were many scattered bands of Delawares, several of which were Christian and at peace with the settlers.

Three years earlier ninety Christian Indians were massacred by settlers from the Pennsylvania border. These martyrs from the Moravian Mission all met their deaths, men, women and children alike. Brother David Zeisberger, missionary to them, had a monument erected in the dead ones' honors.

Some of the Delaware chiefs acknowledged in the Treaty of 1785 at Fort McIntosh had served in the Revolutionary War for the Americans. Those chiefs were Kelelamand or Lt. Colonel Henry, Hengue Pushees or the Big Cat, and Wicocalind or Captain White Eyes.

The main tribe of Delawares, at Grand Blaze, with 480 warriors, was hostile and 480 under Buckongahelas were at the defeat of St. Clair in 1791. But four years later, they joined the peace treaty at Greenville. Signing that treaty for the Delawares at Sandusky were: Hawkinpumiska, Peyamawksey and Rentueco of the Six Nations.

Other Delaware leaders who signed were: Tetabokshke or Grand Glaize King, Lemantanquis or Black King, Wabatthoe, Maghpiway or Red Feather, Kikthawenund or

Anderson, Kishkopekund or Captain Buffalo, Amenahehan or Captain Crow, Queshawksey or George Washington, Weywinquis or Billy Siscomb and Moses.

Delaware leaders who signed for the tribe in 1805 were Puckconsittond, Paahmehelot, Pamoxet or Armstrong, and Pappellelond or Beaver Hat.

In 1808 there were 800 Delaware at Wapeminskink, a few at Sandusky, a few on the Muskingum, and a large body at Fairfield, Canada.

In 1817 the Delaware on the Sandusky were involved in the Treaty signed at the Rapids of the Miami. Jeeshawau or James Armstrong and Sanondoyourayquaw or Silas Armstrong received tracts near that of the Wyandots.

Other Delaware leaders who signed were Kithtuwheland or Anderson, Punchhuck or Capt. Beaver, Tahunqeccoppi or Capt. Pipe, Clamatonockis and Aweallesa or Whirlwind.

Other Delawares who received tracts in that provision were: Captain Pipe, Zeshauau or James Armstrong, Mahawtoo or John Armstrong, Sanowdoyeasquaw or Silas Armstrong, Teorow or Black Raccoon, Hawdorowwatistie or Billy Montour, Buck Wheat, William Dondee, Thomas Lyons, Johnny Cake, Captain Wolf, Isaac Hill, Tishatahoones or widow Armstrong, Ayenucere, Hoomaurow or John Ming and Youdorast.

In 1818 the Delawares, 1800 strong, ceded their lands to the United States and emigrated to Missouri. Those receiving special tracts of land were: a half section, Isaac Wobby, Samuel Cassman, Elizabeth Petchaka and Jacob Dick. One quarter section each was given to Solomon Tindell and Benoni Tindell. Chiefs and warriors representing the tribe who signed the treaty were: Kithteeleland or Anderson, Lapaphnihe or Big Bear, James Nanticoke, Apacahund or White Eyes, Captain Killbuck, The Beaver, Netahopuna, Captain Tunis, Captain Ketchum, The Cat, Ben Beaver, The War Mallet, Captain Caghkoo, The Buck, Petchenanalas, Johnnycake, Quenaghtoothmait and Little Jack.

In 1829, many went to Kansas, and some south of the Red River. At that time on the Little Sandusky, the Delaware chiefs were: Captain Pipe, William Montour, Captain Wolf, Eli Pipe, Solomon Johnnycake, Joseph Armstrong and George Williams. In 1853, they sold all their lands to the United States, except that in Kansas. In 1866, they became citizens, though their clans -- Turtle, Turkey and Wolf -- still exist. 170 of them served in the Civil War.

THE MIAMIS
CHAPTER EIGHT

August 3, 1795 Treaty with the Miamis, Wyandots, Delawares, Shawnees, Ottawas, Chippewas, Potawatomis, Eel-River, Weas, Kickapoos, Piankashaws and Kaskaskias at Greenville, Ohio. Boundaries established between tribal lands and the United States.

October 6, 1818 Treaty with the Miamis concluded at St. Mary's, Ohio. Creation of tribal tracts in Ohio and in Indiana. Rivers established boundaries.

November 28, 1840 Treaty with the Miamis concluded at the Forks of the Wabash, Indiana. Ceded the remainder of the tribal lands in Indiana for land west of the Mississippi.

Early accounts list six divisions of the Miami: Wea, Piankshaw, Atchatchakangouen, Kilatika, Pepicokia and Mengakonkia. The Miami, an Algonquian tribe, have been given many names by other tribes. One is "Omaumeg," a Chippewa term meaning the "who live on the peninsula." The Cherokee called the Miami "Twaatwaa" or crane; the Iroquois said "Twoittois"; the British explorers spelled their name "Twightwees."

Some of the totem of the Miamis were the crane -- that of the Atchatchakangouen -- bear, elk and turtle, but some Miami later insisted that their own name was "MeeMeea," meaning pigeon. Clan groups within the Miami are said to be the wolf, loon, eagle, buzzard, panther, turkey, raccoon, snow, sun and water.

The first time the French came into actual contact with the Miami was when Perrot visited them about 1668. His second visit was in 1670 when they were living at the headwaters of the Fox River in Wisconsin.

Soon after this the Miami parted from the Mascoutens and formed new settlements at the southern end of Lake Michigan and on the Kalamazoo River in Michigan.

The chief village of the Miami on the St. Joseph River formed one part of the tribe and the others were located in northeast Illinois and northern Indiana. As the Miami and their allies were found later on the Wabash in Indiana and in northwest Ohio in which latter territory they gave their name to three rivers, it would seem that they had moved southeast from the localities where first known.

Probably as a result of British influence, the Miami had founded villages on the Maumee River before 1710. By 1751 the Miami had established a large village called Pickawillany about two and a half miles north of the present town of Piqua, Ohio.

It was situated on the northwest side of the Big Miami River, about 150 miles from its mouth, and consisted of approximately 400 families who were augmented daily by new arrivals. This was considered to be one of the strongest Miami towns and it was able to withstand the onslaughts of the Six Nations until about 1763 when the Miami withdrew into Indiana, leaving much of their Ohio lands in the hands of the Shawnee.

In all treaty negotiations the Miami were considered as original owners of the Wabash country and all of western Ohio, while the other tribes in that region were regarded as tenants or intruders on their lands.

By 1795 at the Treaty of Greenville, the Miamis were

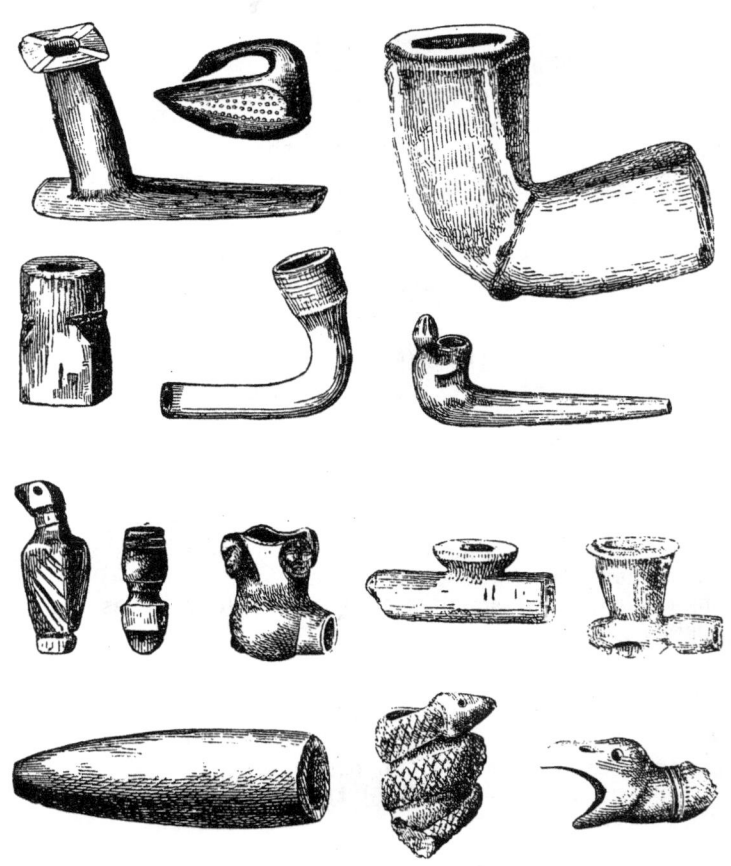

STONE AND CLAY PIPES.

given a specific tract of land within Ohio's borders. Signing that document for the various Miami groups in Ohio were: Nagohquagogh or Le Gris, Meshekunnoghquoh or Little Turtle, Peejeewa or Richardville, Cochkepoghtogh, Shamekunnesa or Soldier, Wapamangwa or White Loon, Amacunca or Little Beaver, Acoolatha or Little Fox and Francis.

They again were involved in the peace treaty signed at Greenville in 1814 when the United States sought peace among the various tribes.

Some of the same individuals received tracts on the Indiana reservations established in 1818 concluded at St. Mary's, Ohio. Chief Jean Baptiste Richardville received three sections of land, and other Miamis by blood who received parcels were: Joseph Richardville and Joseph Richardville, Jr.; Wemetche or the Crescent; Keenquatakqua or Long Hair; Aronzon or Twilight; Peconbequa or a Woman Striking; Aughquamauda or Difficulty; Miaghqua or Noon; Francois Godfroy; Louis Godfroy; Charley, a Miami chief; children of Peter Langlois; children of Antoine Bondie; Francois Lafontaine and son; children of Antoine Rivarre; Peter Labadie; son of George Hunt; Meshenoqua or Little Turtle; Josette Beaubien; Ann Turner, half Miami; Rebecca Hackley, half Miami; William Wayne Wells, half Miami; Mary Wells, half Miami; and Jane Turner Wells, half Miami.

Chieftains who signed the agreement for the Miami were: Peshawa or Richardville, Osas, Ketauga or Charley, Metche Keteta or Big Body, Notawas, Wapapeslea, Tathtenouga, Papskeecha or Flat Belly, Metosma, Sasakuthka or Sun, Keosakunga, Koehenna, Sinamahon or Stone Eater, Cabma, Ameghqua, and Nawaushea.

Finally in 1840, all the Miami including those of Indiana moved west of the Mississippi. In 1867 they were granted the right to merge with the Peoria and others if they so desired.

THE OTTAWAS
CHAPTER NINE

January 21, 1785 Treaty with the Ottawas, Wyandots, Delawares and Chippewas concluded at Fort McIntosh. Boundaries established between tribal lands and the United States.

August 3, 1795 Treaty with the Ottawas, Wyandots, Delawares, Shawnees, Chippewas, Potawatomis, Miamis, Eel-River, Weas, Kickapoos, Piankashaws and Kaskaskias at Greenville, Ohio. Boundaries clarified between tribal lands and that of the United States.

July 4, 1805 Treaty with the Ottawas, Wyandots, Chippewas, Munsees, Delawares, Shawnees and Pottawatomis concluded at Fort Industry on the Miami. Tribe ceded larger portion of tracts for smaller tracts.

November 17, 1807 Treaty with the Ottawas, Chippewas, Wyandots and Pottawatomis made at Detroit, Michigan. Boundaries of tribal lands northwest of the Ohio River re-established.

September 29, 1817 Treaty with the Ottawas, Wyandots, Senecas, Delawares, Shawnees, Pottawatomis and Chippewas concluded at the Rapids of the Miami. Additional cessions of tribal lands made to the United States.

September 17, 1818 Treaty with the Ottawas, Wyandots, Senecas, Shawnees, Delawares, Pottawatomis and Chippewas made at St. Mary's, Ohio. Tracts conveyed in 1817 strictly for tribal use, and additional reservations created.

August 30, 1831 Treaty with the Ottawas concluded at the Rapids of the Miami. Tribe ceded their Ohio lands to the United States for that west of the Mississippi.

Ottawa is translated as meaning "to buy and sell" -- a tribe of Algonquian origins, first found along the Upper Ottawa River in Canada. They were steadfast allies of the French, and at one time closely associated with the Potawatomi and Chippewa to form the confederacy of "The Three Fires."

The Ottawas believed they were derived from three families, each composed of 500 persons. The first was that Michabou or the Great Hare who was a gigantic man who laid nets in 18 fathoms of water which reached only to his armpits and who was born in the island of Michilimackinac, and formed the earth and invented fish-nets after carefully watching a spider weaving its web for taking flies. Among other things he decreed that his descendants should burn their dead and scatter their ashes in the air, for if they failed to do this, the snow would cover the ground continuously and the lakes would remain frozen.

The second family was that of the Namepich or Carp which having spawned its eggs on the shore of the river and the sun casting its rays on them, a woman was thus formed from whom they claimed descent.

The third family was that of the Bear's paw but no explanation was given of the manner in which its genesis took place. But when a bear was killed, a feast of its own flesh was given in its honor.

The Ottawas were allies and firm friends of the French and the Hurons or Wyandots, and conducted an active trade between the western tribes and the French.

Soon after 1649, they fled before the Iroquois to Green Bay, thence west beyond the Mississippi to the country of the Sioux, with whom they became involved in war, when they fell back to Chegoimegon before 1660, and finally to Mackinaw.

The tribe became considerably divided here, one of the divisions settling near Detroit, and the one at Mackinaw passing over to Arbe Croche. The greater number of the Ottawa were in the last war with the French, and at its close Pontiac, an Ottawa chief, one of the ablest leaders of any tribe that ever lived, organized a vast conspiracy for the destruction of the English.

They were under the British influence during the Revolution. At the treaty of peace at Greenville in 1795, they agreed to boundaries with the other tribes -- theirs being a certain tract of land on the Miami River. Signing that treaty in 1795 for the Ottawa were: Augooshaway, Keenoshameek, La Malice, Machiwetah, Thowonawa, Secaw and Chegonickska, an Ottawa from Sandusky.

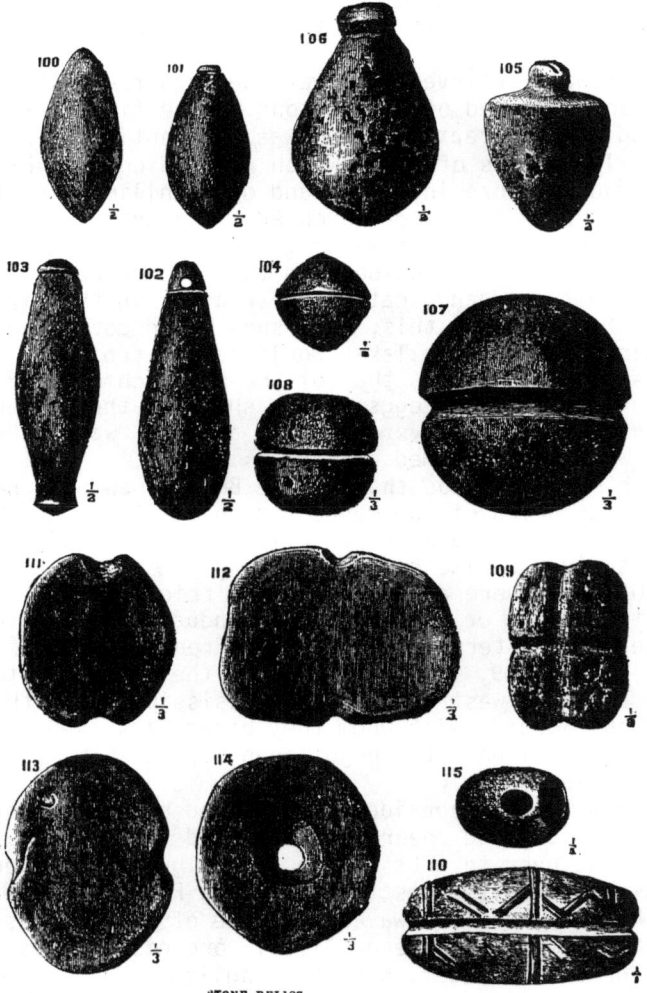

STONE RELICS.

In the Treaty of 1805, the Ottawa's tract was drawn on the south shore of Lake Erie. Ottawa chieftains who signed that agreement at that time were: Nekeik or Little Otter, Kawachewan or Eddy, Mechimenduch or Big Bowl, Aubaway, Ogonse, Sawgamaw, Tusqugan or McCarty, Tondawganie or the Dog and Ashawet.

Again in 1807 the boundaries for those tracts were re-establlished for the Ottawa. Individuals involved in that agreement were: Aubauway, Kawachewan, Sawgamaw, Ogouse and Wasagashick.

In the treaty reached in 1817, the Ottawa were granted the use of a tract of land on Blanchard's Fork of the Great Auglaize River, five miles square, and another tract, three miles square, including Oquanoxa's village.

Special allotments were granted to Anthony Shane, a half Ottawa, who received one section of land on the east side of St. Mary's River, and Peter Minor, an adopted son of Tondaganie or the Dog, who received a section of land on the north side of the Miami at the Wolf Rapid. The tribe retained their tract on the south side of the Miami River of Lake Erie which included Tushquegan or M'Carty's village.

Other Ottawas who signed the agreement were: Tontagimi or the Dog, Misquegin or McCarty, Pontiac, Oquenoxas, Tashmwa, Nowkesick, Wabekeighke, Kinewaba, Twaatum, Supay, Nashkema, Kuwashewon and Kusha.

In 1831 the Ottawa ceeded their land in Ohio to the United States for land west of the Mississippi. The Ottawa chiefs requested special tracts to remain in the hands of certain individuals in the state of Ohio. One of the chiefs Waubegakake was to receive a temporary lease on a tract for three years adjoining the section granted and occupied by Yellow Hair or Peter Minor. Muckquiona or Bearskin was also to retain a tract on or near the Maumee River.

Hiram Thebeault, half Ottawa, and William McNabb, half Ottawa, were each given tracts. Others who signed the agreement were: Artaishnaiwan, Oquainaasa, Oschano or Charlo, Quacint, Wawbagacake, Checauk, Petonoquet, Oshawwanon, Penaiswe, Nauquagasheek, Penaiswonquet, Peshekeinee, Cumchaw of Blanchard's Fork, Cumchaw of Wolf Rapids, Susain, Cabayaw, Oshoquene, Muccotaipeenaisee, Osage, Pantee, Mesaukee, Omussenau, Nondaiwau and Eauvaince.

VILLAGES AND TRAILS
CHAPTER TEN

Bands of warriors, in passing up and down, used one of two trails in Ohio; the one west of the Big Miami, the other east of the Little Miami River, running north from the Ohio River to the Shawnee towns, at Old Chillicothe (three miles north of Xenia), the Piqua towns on the Mad River, 17 miles above Dayton, and on up to the Mackacheek towns at the head waters of Mad River; the trail to the west from the Ohio below the mouth of the Big Miami leading on up, passing west of Hamilton, just east of Eaton, through Fort Jefferson and Greenville, to the portage at Loramie, and branching from there to the villages north and west.

Other trails which formed a "trunk line" crossed the Muskingum River in the vicinity of Zanesville, passing a little south of west across Perry and Fairfield Counties, but wholly south of Licking, A branch trail, however, diverged from this main trail, crossed the Muskingum in the vicinity of the present site of Dresden, and striking Licking County, about where Licking River passes out of it, on the east passed up that river to the vicinity of Bowling Green, where it crossed and bore southwest to the "Big" and "Little" lakes, or what is now the reservoir. This trail passed on from the reservoir to King Beaverstown, near Pickerington or Lithopolis, in Fairfield County, near the head-waters of the Hock-Hocking.

The trails leading south on the east side of the Little Miami and on the east side of the Big Miami were constantly used by the hunters, while they were supplied with meat by parties in the valleys. They would cross the Ohio, attack small settlements in Kentucky, carry off prisoners and plunder, retreat rapidly and thus escape punishment. In 1778, Daniel Boone was captured in Kentucky by one of these parties and taken to the Shawnee town at Old Chillicothe, near Xenia. In the summer of the same year, these tribes formed an expedition of 450 strong to attack Boonesboro, Kentucky. Boone escaped from them and notified the inhabitants of their coming.

In 1773 the chief town of the Shawnees was Chillicathee on which nearby plain they raised their cornfields which supplied most of their food and their houses were made of logs. About three miles west and north from

Chillicaathee was a small town called Wockachaalli which signified "Crooked Noses Place." It was situated on the east side of Paint Creek where the tribe had a large number of excellent horses and a substantial herd of livestock from which they obtained most of their food.

Grenadier Squawtown and Cornstalk's town near on Scippo Creek, a tributary of the Scioto, were also nearby. At the mouth of the Scioto was Shaneetown which in 1751 contained forty houses on the south side of the Ohio and about a hundred houses on the north side with a kind of a state house (council) about ninety feet long with a tight cover of bark.

Hurricane Tom's town was upon the Scioto very near the present northern boundary of Pike county. The word Scioto signified Hairy River as the tribes found that the deer were so plentiful when they first settled here that the stream would be thick of hairs of the deer who drank the water.

The old tribal town of Piqua was situated about five miles west of the present site of the city of Springfield, Ohio, on the north bank of Mad River. From this prairie on which the town was located ran the road to Chillicothe which was twelve miles south. Behind the town was a round-topped hill, rising up 100 feet from the level of the plain. From the crown of this hill, the country might be overlooked for as much as four miles up and down the river.

In 1780 Piqua was quite populous and at one time contained nearly four thousand Shawnees. The town was built after the manner of French villages. The houses extended along the river more than three miles, and were in many places more than 20 poles apart.

The word "Piqua" signifies a man formed out of ashes, such as the Phoenix. The first Piqua was in Clark County which later became the town of New Boston. The Shawnees moved to later Miami County and formed a village there also known as Piqua. And there was a third location in later Pickaway County.

The tribes had two villages within the present limits of Licking County. The Delawares and Shawnees jointly occupied one situated on the Bowling Green, four miles below the junction of the North and South Forks. The other was a Wyandot village called Raccoontown, and was situated on Raccoon Creek, a short distance from Johnstown in the present township of Monroe. The tribe sold their town to Charles and George Green in 1807 and immediately abandoned it though a remnant of them remained within the

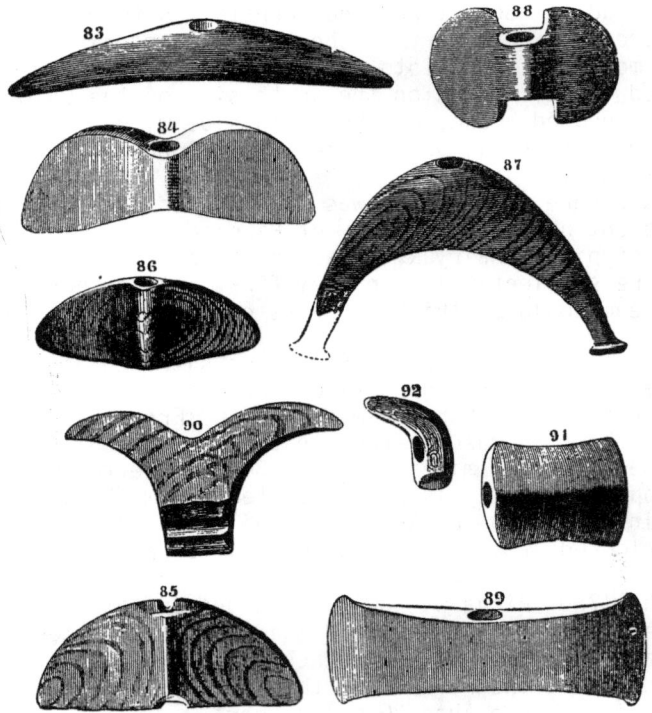

DRILLED CEREMONIAL WEAPONS OF SLATE.
Fig. 87 is a *fac-simile* of a double crescent, owned by Gen. R. Brinkerhoff, at Newville.

county some years later.

The most noted tribal town in later Richland County was that of Greentown, section 18 of Green township. Greentown was started about 1783 which was named for Thomas Green, companion to Jelloway, Armstrong, Billy Montour and Tom Lyons. The tribes remained here until 1812 where they held many feasts, cultivated fields of corn adjacent to the village, built cabins, and entertained.

Jeromeville, another important tribal town in this area of Ohio, was founded by John Baptiste Jerome, a Canadian Frenchman who came about 1784 to the Huron River where he married a sister of the known tribal leader George Hamilton. After marriage, Jerome removed to the upper Sandusky where he remained until the outbreak of the hostilities in 1790 when he and Captian Pipe engaged in battle with the Americans.

After the treaty of Greenville, Jerome, Capt. Pipe and a number of Delawares came to the site of Mohican Johnstown on the south side of the stream about three-quarters of a mile from the present Jeromeville where they established a town. This was about 1802 or 1803.

Jerome crossed the stream and built a cabin a little northeast of a mill site long afterward used for such. He was here when the first settlers came and had considerable land cleared in the creek bottoms. He resided in this cabin with his wife and daughter until the tribe was removed by orders of Capt. Murray. The removal caused their death. He was never the same man again. He married a German woman, sold his farm, and after one or two moves, died at his old home on the Huron River.

Another old tribal town in Richland County was Helltown which was not far from the present village of Newville.

A celebrated war-path, extending from Sandusky to Beaver (Fort McIntosh), passed through Summit County. This was the trail traversed by the tribes of northern Ohio in their expeditions against the border settlements in Pennsylvania. The trail crossed the Cuyahoga in Franklin Township, Portage County, at what is called "Standing Stone," and divided at Fish Creek, the northern branch extending across Stow and Northampton Townships to the tribal village in the latter, thence across the river to the Mingo village in Bath, and thence westward, while the southern branch extending somewhat south of west, led to the villages at Cuyahoga Falls, thence on through Portage and Coventry, to the Tuscarawas River and the Delaware village in Coventry.

When the Delaware villages in Summit County were first established is not definitely known but from an old map which was published in 1755 by Lewis Evans, there was a Mingo village on the west bank of the river, probably in what is now eastern Bath, and an Ottawa village on the opposite side of the river in Northampton or in Boston.

When the American settlers appeared, this area was occupied by the Ottawas under their chief Stigwanish, while a half-mile northwest was a Seneca village under the chief Ponty. There were two other tribal towns, in early years, at Cuyahoga Falls. On the north side of the river was a town of Delawares, and on the south, one of the Iroquois.

The only village of the Hurons or Wyandots known to exist in later Richland County or in the edge of Crawford County at a place called Knisely's Spring later Annapolis.

In 1763 the Miamis towns were called "Tewightewee towns" found on the Upper Piqua. The Miamis left this area and the Shawnees moved in.

In the early days, a tribal trail ran from the site of Franklinton to Old Chillicothe (north of Xenia). It passed through the present site of Georgesville, Franklin County, thence in a southwest direction to the large spring in Oak Run Township, subsequently known as "Springer's Spring," thence to Old Chillicothe.

The same trail was later called "Chenoweth's trace" named for two brothers as early as 1799. Two other trails are known to have passed through Madison County: one up the banks of the Big Darby, and another from the tribal towns on the Scioto, to those on Mad River, and the Big and Little Miami Rivers, passing through the site of London, in a northwesterly direction.

BIOGRAPHIES
CHAPTER ELEVEN

Blackhoof or Cutthewekasaw

Of the many distinguished chiefs in Indian history there are but few, who rank higher in prowess, bravery, and wisdom in council, than did Blackhoof, chief of the Shawnee tribes. He was born in Florida, in 1711, and afterward lived in the Carolinas until the Shawnees emigrated to the Cumberland Valley. In that valley he grew to manhood. When the tribes afterward obtained permission to occupy certain portions of the Ohio Territory, he accompanied them to the Miami Valley.

The cabin in which he lived for many years was located on the west bank of the Miami River, a short distance south of the mouth of Loramie creek near a spring, known at the present day as Blackhoof's Spring. There he continued to reside until General Clark made his celebrated raid on the Mad River and Piqua towns. After the destruction of their villages, the Shawnees retreated to localities further north and west. The tribe to which Blackhoof was attached was located at Wapakoneta.

Blackhoof or Cutthewekasaw was present with other tribes of Shawnees, at the defeat of General Braddock, near Pittsburgh in 1755. In that battle and other engagements that followed soon afterward, he so distinguished himself for his desperation, and military ability, that he became known far and wide.

Colonel Johnston is the authority for the statement that Blackhoof had probably been in more battles than any living man of his day. He led war parties in their attacks on boats, descending the Ohio river near Pittsburgh to Cincinnati, in which many lives were lost, and many captives were led to Shawnee towns. He commanded 150 warriors at St. Clair's defeat, and participated in the battle of the Fallen Timbers.

After the defeat of the allied Indian nations by Wayne, Blackhoof and his band of Shawnee warriors returned to Wapakoneta. Later, Blackhoof and his trusted followers established themselves at Blackhoof-Town, now the site of the flourishing village of St. Johns. There, on the summit of a mound that afforded an extensive view of the surrounding country, he built a cabin in which he lived until his death, in the summer of 1831.

Blackhoof is said to have been opposed to polygamy and the practice of burning prisoners. He lived forty years with one wife, raising a large family of children, who both loved and respected him. He was small in stature, not more than five feet eight inches in height. He was favored with good health and unimpaired eye-sight to the period of his death.

Quaskey, his eldest son, possessed many of the qualities of his distinguished father. He went west with his people in 1832 and died about 1869. He, like his father, was a good speaker.

The description of the funeral ceremonies at the burial of Blackhoof was preserved in "Harvey's History of the Shawnees." Harvey and his wife was present, by invitation. He says, "Being present upon that occasion, I was very much struck with the solemn and disconsolate appearance of all classes of the Shawnees. They had for many years looked to the experienced chief, in peace and war. He was of such an age that recollections carried him back to the men who had, in 1682, made the great treaty at Philadelphia, and with a clear recollection of these transactions, encouraged the people of his nation in becoming a civilized people."

Roundhead

The Wyandot chief, Roundhead, had a village on the Scioto in the southwest corner of Hardin County, where the town of Round Head was subsequently laid out. At what precise date the Indians started this village is not known, but about the year 1800 Maj. James Galloway, of Greene County, visited them at this point, and says that there was then quite a number of apple trees in the village and that the Indians raised many swine.

Some of those trees, said to have been planted by this old chief, are yet standing. Roundhead, whose Indian name was Stiahta, was fine looking man. He had a brother named John Battise, a man of great size and personal strength. He was well remembered by the pioneers of the Miami and Scioto Valleys on account of possessing an enormous nose, which resembled in size and hue an immense blue potato full of indentations, and when he laughed, it shook like jelly.

He lived at a place called Battisetown some miles west of his brother's village, joined the British in 1812, and was killed at the siege of Fort Meigs. In 1807 Roundhead was present with Tecumseh and other chiefs at a council held at Springfield, Ohio, between the settlers and Indians to settle a difficulty which arose over the killing of a individual named Meyers, a few miles west of Urbana. The execution of Leather Lips, a well-known Wyandot chief, which took place twelve miles north of Columbus, Ohio, in 1810, on the trumped-up charge of witchcraft, was intrusted by Tecumseh to Roundhead, who at the head of six braves came from Tippecanoe and did the deed.

Captain Pipe

Captain Pipe, one of the principal chiefs of the Delawares and for a long time after 1795, was a fervent friend of the settlers. He had been an inveterate foe, and was the principal actor in the cruel execution of Col. Crawford, in retaliation for the wanton murder of their Moravian brothers, ninety of them.
This was in strict accord with the ideas of Indian justice, and had Col. Williamson, the commander of the militia who so cruelly slew the inoffensive Moravians, been captured, Col. Crawford would have been spared.
Capt. Pipe seemed to accept the results of war, and, knowing that the power of the Indians was gone, lived peaceably until his death. He was one of the Indian chiefs who signed the treaty of peace at Greenville, July 22, 1814, between the United States and his and other tribes.
By this act he fully identified himself with the American cause. When he came to Mohican John's town or Mohican Johnstown, as it is variously written, he built his cabin about one mile northwest of the old Mingo town, south of the stream, and on what is now the Haysville road. There he lived several years. Capt. Pipe was described to be humane, fine looking, dignified, courteous, a magnificent specimen of physical manhood, fully six feet high, and exceptionally well-proportioned. The cabin in which he lived was about twelve feet square, and was well made.

The Armstrong Family

The Armstrong family of Indians, members of the Delaware nation, became better known among the settlers than any other family. Thomas Armstrong was the chief of

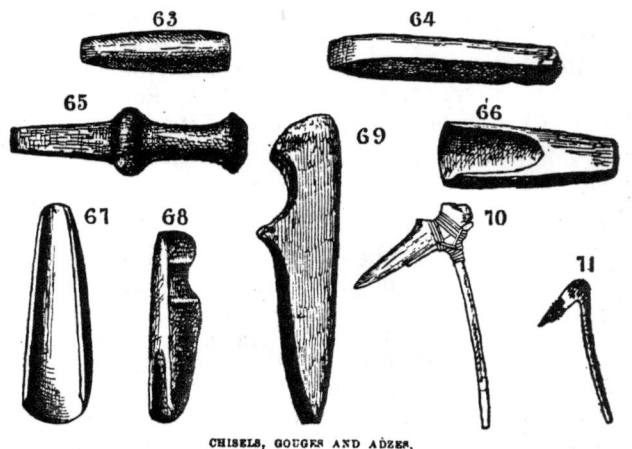

CHISELS, GOUGES AND ADZES.

the Delawares at Greentown, and their leader against the Americans in the Indian wars between 1790 and 1795. He was associated with Capt. Pipe, leader of the Delawares, upon the Sandusky and Huron Rivers.

Both were defeated by Gen. Wayne, whose power they ever after feared. After the treaty of peace at Greenville, Capt. Pipe, with Jerome and others, came to Richland County and established Jeromeville.

Thomas Armstrong must have died sometime before 1817 as he is not a signer for that treaty but there are other Armstrongs, including a Widow Armstrong, who are mentioned in that treaty. Quite possibly his son, John M. Armstrong studied law and married Lucy Bigelow, daughter of Rev. Russell Bigelow. He later went to Upper Sandusky and became chief of his tribe. He regulated their affairs, did much to elevate them, and while there was associated with Chub, Monque, Blue Eyes, Between the Logs, and other noted Indians.

The Indians were Methodists, and supported a church established by Rev. James B. Finley about 1820. The mission church building was built of blue limestone, in

1824, from government funds. The church still remained in 1880, and around it the graves of many of the Indian converts.

Captain Logan or Tahgahjute

Logan was the second son of Shikellimus or Shikellamy, a celebrated chief who lived upon the Susquehanna. His Indian name was Tahgahjute, and he was named in English after James Logan, the secretary of Pennsylvania, of whom his father was firm friend and great admirer.

Logan, being driven from his home in Pennsylvania, came to Ohio in 1772, and at first located at a Mingo village on the Ohio River, at the mouth of Indian Cross Creek.

After the surrender of Detroit in 1812, it soon became apparent that an attack would be made on Fort Wayne. At that time there were many women and children in the garrison, who in case of an attack, would have been detrimental to its defense, and it therefore became necessary to have them speedily removed to a place of safety.

By order of military authorities, Colonel Johnston of Piqua assembled the Shawnee chiefs, and stating the case requested volunteers to bring the women and children from Fort Wayne to Piqua. Logan immediately arose and offered his services, and soon started with a party of mounted Indians, all volunteers.

They reached the post, received their interesting and helpless charge, and safetly brought them to the settlement through a country infested with marauding bands of Indians. The women spoke in the highest terms of the vigilance, care and delicacy of their faithful conductors. It is said that Logan did not sleep from the time that he left Piqua until he returned.

Logan and two other Shawnees acted as scouts for General Harrison's march to Fort Wayne which was under siege. Before they got there however, the enemy made a hasty retreat.

Again for General Harrison, Logan, his friends Captain Johnny and Brighthorn, were directed to scout out the territory on the Maumee near Fort Defiance. Logan and his friends barely escaped with their lives when they encountered the enemy. Logan and his companions managed to kill five out of the seven British party.

Logan was wounded and lived two days after reaching camp, in extreme bodily pain. He was buried, with the honors of war, within the inclosure of Fort Winchester to prevent his enemies from disinterring the body to obtain his scalp.

Logan left a dying request that his two sons be sent to Kentucky, and there educated and brought up under the care of Colonel Hardin. After peace was made with the Indians, neither the chiefs or Logan's widow would comply by sending the boys to Frankfort, Kentucky where Hardin lived.

Finally the chiefs and widow consented to let Colonel Johnston take the boys to Piqua to be schooled. The widow and mother would not let the boys learn. They emigrated to the west with the rest of the tribe.

LOGAN'S SPEECH.

"I appeal to any white man to say if he ever entered Logan's cabin hungry and he gave him not meat; if ever he came cold and naked, and he clothed him not.

"During the course of the last, long and bloody war, Logan remained idle in his cabin an advocate for peace. Such was my love for the whites, that my countrymen pointed as they passed and said, 'Logan is the friend of the white man.' I had even thought to live with you, but for the injuries of one man. Colonel Cresap,* the last spring, in cold blood, and unprovoked, murdered all of the relatives of Logan, not even sparing my women and children. There runs not a drop of my blood in the veins of any living creature. This called on me for revenge. I have sought it. I have killed many. I have fully glutted my vengeance. For my country I rejoice at the beams of peace. But do not harbor a thought that mine is the joy of fear. Logan never felt fear. He will not turn on his heel to save his life. Who is there to mourn for Logan? Not one."

Wathethewela or Bright Horn

Wathethewela or Bright Horn, was another noted chief, who was present when Logan was mortally wounded in the contest with Winemac in 1812, and was severely wounded in the thigh in the same fight, but recovered and lived at Wapakonetta.

He was, with Blackhoof, the especial friend of Gen. Harrison, in the war of 1812. He was a brave man, and of sound integrity. He fought like a hero, was a large and commanding Indian in appearance, and was quite shrewd and intelligent.

His cabin stood on the north bank of Quaker Run, near the site of the Distlerath slaughterhouse of later years. He is said to have died at Wapakoneta in 1825 or 1826.

Peter Cornstalk

The Indian chieftain, Peter Cornstalk, was born at Old Chillicothe about 1751, and was the son of the celebrated chief of that name who was assassinated at Point Pleasant in 1774. Like his father, Peter Cornstalk was commanding in appearance, and had the lofty bearing of the true Indian.

He fought in the battles against Harmar, St. Clair and Wayne, hoping to retain his country. But when finally defeated in 1794, he decided that further resistance was useless, and signed the Treaty of Greenville in 1795.

After the expulsion of the Indians from Piqua by General Clark, he and his tribe settled on the east bank of the Auglaize River about two miles below Wapakoneta, where he resided until he and his tribe moved to Kansas.

At the age of 82 years, Cornstalk accompanied his tribe to Kansas, and settled on the Kansas River. A son Nernpeneshequah also went with him in 1832. Cornstalk lived until about the year 1845. He was buried in the Quaker Mission cemetery near the Kansas River.

Cornstalk

Cornstalk was the greatest chief among the Scioto Shawnees. He was great in war but foremost in making peace. If he led in battle, his voice sounding from the front, "Be strong! Be strong!" incited the warriors to their utmost efforts, and if he counseled peace, his words were equally potent.

Cornstalk and Red Hawk went over to the American fort opposite Point Pleasant in the early summer of 1777 to talk matters over with Captain Arkbuckle about the British agents who were stirring up the Indians. Both the chiefs knew Arkbuckle and felt that they could talk with him.

The Americans knowing that the Shawnees were inclining to the enemy, thought it would be a good plan to detain Cornstalk and Red Hawk as hostages. The old chief finding himself entrapped, calmly awaited the result. Ellenipsco, the son of Cornstalk, who came the next morning to see his father, was also detained.

Toward night one of the American hunters having been shot by an unknown Indian, the soldiers raised a cry, "Kill the red dogs in the fort," and immediately carried their bloody thought into execution, the commander endeavoring, though almost unheeded, to dissuade them from their purpose.

The chietain saw his assassinators coming, and met them at the door of the hut, in which he was confined, his arms folded upon his massive chest, and his whole mien expressing a most magnificent stoicism.

His son, Ellenipsco, trembled violently. Cornstalk encouraged him to meet his fate composedly, saying, "My son, the Great Spirit has sent you here that we may died together." Cornstalk fell pierced by seven musket balls. Ellenipsco saw his father sink bleeding before him, but continued still and passive, not even rising from his seat. He met his death with the utmost calmness. Red Hawk suffered a similar fate.

The Shawnees who were at peace were again at war after this incident.

Buckongahelas

Buckongahelas or Shingess was supposed to have been born near Philadelphia after a few years of the treaties with Penn. In colonial days, with Jacobs and other leading Delawares, he resided in western Pennsylvania, and is believed at that time to have been identical with the "Shingess" who entertained George Washington, when a young man in 1753.

Washington called upon him to invite him to council at the Logtown. Shingess at first attended, but afterward made his wife's sickness an excuse for absence.

Shingess was an active warrior when Fort Du Quesne was taken in 1759. Heckewelder speaks of meeting him a the Tuscarora town on the Muskingum as early as 1762. He stated, "Passing a day with him in the summer of 1762, at Tuscarora, on the Muskingum, near by where his two prisoner boys (about 12 years of age) were amusing themselves with his own boys, and he observed me looking that way, inquired what I was looking at. On my replying that I was looking at his prisoners, he said 'When I first took them they were such, but they are now my children; eat their victuals out of the same bowl,' which was saying as much as that they, in all respects, were on an equal footing with his own children."

Shortly before Bouquet's expedition to the Muskingum, Shingess or Buckongalhelas moved to the west, and settled on the Maumee River. Later he moved up the Auglaize River and located at the Ottawa towns near Fort Amanda.

He and his tribe of warriors participated in the battles of Harmar, St. Clair and Wayne.

Buckongahelas was not only a great, but a noble warrior. He took no delight in shedding blood. He had been so much under the influence of the Moravian missionaries.

In 1792 when Colonel Hardin, Major Truman and others were sent in May of that year by President Washington with a flag of truce to the Indian nations of the west, they were taken prisoners by a party of Indians who treated them well at first and made many professions of friendship, but in the end took advantage of them, except William Smalley, who was conducted to Buckongahelas.

Buckongahelas chastised the men for murdering the truce carriers as he told them that they had no way of escape, and that they were only interested in the personal effects on the carriers. The chief took Smalley into his cabin, and kept him as a guest for near a month, as he feared some young Indians would do harm to Smalley.

The chief signed the Greenville treaty in 1795 and all the subsequent treaties up to August 18, 1804.

Upon his return to Vincennes, he became sick, and died late in the fall of 1804. He is supposed to have been over a hundred years old.

Blue Jacket or Weyapiersenwaw

Nothing is known of Blue Jacket of his early life with certainty until the defeats of Harmar and St. Clair. In those engagements he served as a subordinate office under Little Turtle. In those two battles, he so distinguished himself that he was made commander-in-chief at the Battle of the Fallen Timbers.

It is said that on the night preceding that battle a council was held in which seven Indian nations were represented. The expediency of attacking Wayne at Presque Isle was then considered. Blue Jacket warmly favored the proposition, and Little Turtle in a speech of much ability opposed it. Blue Jacket's advice and influence, however, prevailed. A battle was fought with desperation, and the Indians were disastrously defeated.

Blue Jacket and the others were greatly discouraged

after their defeat. Many councils were held, resulting in a desire to treat for peace. Preparations were about completed in October, for Blue Jacket, at the head of the deputation of chiefs, to proceed to Greenville to sue for peace, when the mission was arrested by the receipt of a message from Governor Simcoe, inviting him to attend a meeting to be held at the mouth of the Detroit River, on the 10th of October. Blue Jacket consented, which caused a delay of the peace negotiations until the next year.

After the Detroit meeting, he moved to Wapakoneta, and attended the Greenville meeting the next fall. He must have died sometime before 1817 since in that treaty of that year it was indicated that Nancy Stewart, daughter of the late Shawnee chief Blue Jacket was to receive one section of land on the Great Miami River below Lewistown. His sons also received parcels in that treaty.

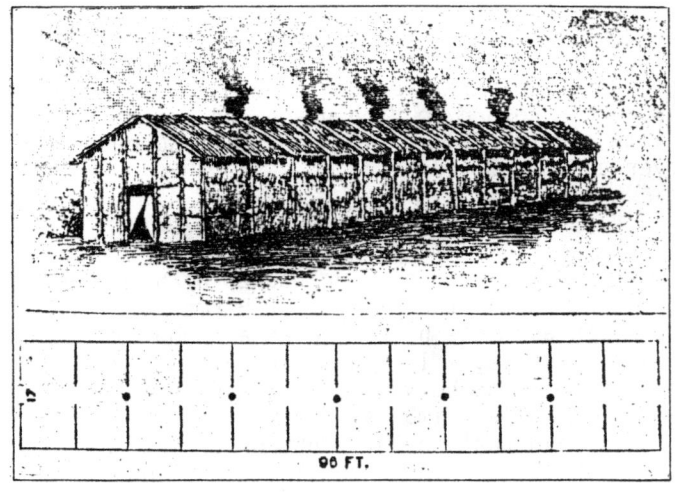

Tecumseh

Tecumseh's place of birth and date are not known with certainty. Some say it was at Piqua, an Indian town, on Mad River. His father's name was Pukeesheno which means, "I light from flying." He was killed in the battle of Kanhawa in 1774. His mother's name was Meetheetashe which signifies, a turtle laying her eggs in the sand. She died among the Cherokees. She had at one birth three sons about (1770?): Tecumseh meaning cougar crouching for his prey; Laulewasikau or Ellskwatawa or Prophet meaning an open door; and Rumskaka or Kumskaukau meaning a tiger that flies in the air.

It is stated that the first battle in which he was engaged, occurred on the site of Dayton between a party of Kentuckians under Colonel Benjamin Logan and some Shawnees. At the age of 17 he accompanied marauding bands of warriors along the Ohio.

Tecumseh was inclined to stoutness, but possessed, withal, the agility, perseverance and endurance, peculiar to Indian warriors. He led a wandering restless life. At later dates he resided at Greenville, at Wapakonetta, at the mouth of the Auglaize River, at Fort Wayne and on the Wabash River.

Tecumseh became prominent as a warrior about 1804 when he began long horseback trips over most of the South, trying to enlist the tribes in his cause. He argued that the United States government had no right to buy land from a single tribe, because the land belonged in common to all tribes. Tecumseh went into Canada several times, and even crossed westward over the Mississippi in his journeys.

At the beginning of the War of 1812, Tecumseh went to Canada where he was highly esteemed. The British commissioned him a brigadier general in their forces.

In the spring of 1811, Tecumseh called for a council with the tribes in the southern part of the country. Accompanied by a party of some thirty braves, he appeared at a gathering of the Choctaws and Chickasaws, and made a plea for them to join in a common effort against the Americans. Tecumseh eloquently made an appeal for unity, and it was evident that he found some of the Choctaws and Chickasaws sympathetic to his appeal.

However, he had not anticipated the hold that Pushmataha, chief of the Choctaws, had upon his people. Pushmataha spoke before the same council, and his answer to the speech of Tecumseh prevented the Choctaws and Chickasaws from joining in what later became the War of

1812.
Tecumseh was killed in the battle on the Thames River, near Chatham, Ontario, on October 5, 1813.

TECUMTHA.

Little Turtle

Little Turtle was born in a village on the Eel River, about 1747. His father was a chieftain of the Miamis, and his mother was a Mohican. Little Turtle became the war chief of the Miamis at an early age. He was rather short in stature, but well built, with symmetrical form. He had a prominent forehead, heavy eyebrows, keen black eyes, and a large chin.
Little Turtle possessed a remarkable mind, and was for years the leading member of the Miamis. He was unsurpassed for bravery and his intelligence was exceeded by no one else of his race. He lost no opportunity to gain new information and knowledge, and he was interested in just about any subject or object that came to his attention. In later life he used his influence to encourage his people to be peaceful, sober and industrious.
Little Turtle was one of the signers of the Treaty of Greenville, Ohio on August 3, 1795. He had also signed

many other treaties in behalf of the Miamis. After signing the Greenville Treaty, Little Turtle remained a faithful friend of the United States.

Little Turtle died July 14, 1812 at his lodge a short distance from the junction of the St. Joseph and the St. Mary Rivers.

John Wolf or Lawatucheh

Lawatucheh was known to all the early traders and pioneers as one of the most upright and reliable of the Indians. He was often employed to transport goods from Piqua to Fort Wayne and other remote points. He frequently accompanied Colonel Johnston at the times of his disbursements of annuities to the different tribes.

His son Henry Clay was named after Henry Clay of Kentucky, and was educated at Upper Piqua under the supervision of Colonel Johnston at the expense of the Quakers. He afterwards became a leading chief, and was a man of considerable talent. He went to Kansas with his tribe, and lived many years after their removal.

During the removal to Kansas, the committee making the disbursements found that they had $20 left. They decided to distribute it equally among the chiefs. The chiefs refused the money and indicated that it should be given to Lawatucheh or John Wolf since he had been sick for a long time, and was unable to purchase a wagon to move west in.

John Wolf never recovered from leaving his home in Ohio, and he died in Kansas, a poor man.

Francis Duchouquet

Francis Duchouquet was the son of a French-Indian trader who was engaged in the trade with the Indians of northern Ohio and Michigan during the occupancy of that region by the French. He was born near Presque Isle in 1751. After reaching manhood, he engaged in the fur trade in which business he visited nearly all the tribes of Ohio and Indiana territories.

In his trips to central Ohio he married a Shawnee woman. After his marriage he lived on Mad River until the Indians were driven from that locality by General Clark. When the Shawnees moved to Wapakoneta, he accompanied them and erected a dwelling-house and other buildings on the north bank of the Auglaize River.

When the Indian tribes of Ohio and Indiana began to

assemble at Greenville in the fall of 1795, Duchouquet was summoned to act as one of the interpreters during the negotiations. Again, he was called in 1817 to serve as an interpreter in the treaty made by Duncan McArthur and Lewis Cass at the foot of the Rapids.

The year following 1818 he for the third time served as an interpreter at the treaties held at St. Marys.

His residence on the north bank of Auglaize River became a house of entertainment at an early date where traveling traders and explorers of the western wilds were always sure of accommodations. His store and warehouse were located at the wharf in front of his residence.

At the close of the fur season, his peltries were deposited on pirouges, and floated down to the mouth of the Auglaize where they were either sold to traders at that point or reshipped to Detroit where they were sold for cash or exchanged for goods. The goods if bought at Detroit were carried on vessels to the mouth of the Auglaize from which point they were transported on packhorses to Wapakoneta.

He continued residing at this location until his death in the fall of 1831.

Tu-Taw

Tu-Taw was a noted scout and mail carrier during the campaigns of Wayne and Harrison between Piqua and Defiance. He was French and Shawnee, being a descendant of an early French trader. He did not accompany the Shawnees when they went west.

He had many hair-breadth escapes during the time that he was a carrier of dispatches between Cincinnati and Wayne's outposts. In one instance he was attacked by a single Indian in which scalping-knives were the instruments of offense and defense. In the encounter the Indian attempted to stab Tu-Taw. He parried the thrust of the Indian with his left hand grasping the murderous arm at the wrist, and dispatched the would-be assassin with his right hand. In the scuffle, however, the Indian succeeded in drawing the knife through his left hand, severing the tendons of three fingers. When the wound healed, the fingers remained stiff.

After the wars were over he made his home with Peter Hammel for a number of years. During one occasion in harvesting wheat with Hammel, Tu-Taw was bitten by a rattle snake between his knee and ankle. Immediately Tu-Taw ran to the nearby river, grabbed some crawfish mud and put it over the wound. He then chewed some stalk of a weed and added its juice to the mudpack. The remedy worked.

The latter portion of Tu-Taw's life was spent in trapping, hunting and fishing. When not engaged in those pursuits, his time was occupied in gardening for his neighbors, a skill in which he was expert. The old patriot died in the 78th year of his age, and was buried in the old Duchouquet Cemetery.

WAYWELEAPY.

Wayweleapy

Wayweleapy was the principal speaker among the Shawnees at the period of their removal. He was an eloquent orator, grave, gay or humorous as occasion required. At times his manner is said to have been quite fascinating, his countenance so full of varied expression and his voice so musical that surveyors and other strangers passing through the country listened to him with delight, although the words fell upon their ears in an unknown language.

During the negotiations for the sale of their reserve at Wapakoneta, he addressed his people and Mr. Gardner several times. His refutation of Gardner's assumed superiority over the Indian race was complete and full of irony.

Henry Harvey in his history of the Shawnees states that "when the time for the removal of the Indians to the west arrived, Gardner desired to take them by way of Bellefontaine, Urbana, Xenia, Lebanon and Lawrenceburgh -- 150 miles further than necessary. The chiefs notified him that they knew the road as well as he did, and would not go that way; that they would go by way of Greenville, Richmond, and Indianapolis. After their refusal to comply with Gardner's request, they were addressed by a disbursing agent, a young man from West Point, who urged them in a speech of considerable length to take Gardiner's advice; that if it was further it would cost them nothing, as the government would pay all expense, and that by going this route they would see several fine towns, farms and many Americans.

"At the conclusion of the speech Wayweleapy arose with great dignity and complimented the young man by saying that he was pleased with his speech, and now he hoped all would be done about right, and that they would have no more trouble. He then turned to Gardner and gravely remarked to him: 'My friend, we, the chiefs are old men; have been in council with such men as Governor Cass and John Johnston: tell the President we don't do business with boys. Now, my friend, I have no more to say.'

"When the speaker concluded his remarks, one general burst of laughter arose from the Indians, as well as the Americans present."

At the age of 80 years this chief accompanied his tribe to Kansas where he died in 1843.

Pht or Fallen Timbers

Pht or Fallen Timbers was the last chief of his tribe in Ohio that survived the battle of Presque Isle. His name was pronounced Pe-aitch-ta.

Under his leadership the council house was built at Shawnee Town in 1831 but it was not completed. His cabin stood but a few rods northwest of the council-house.

Here, after a long sickness, the chief died and was buried a short time before the removal of the Hog Creek Indians to Kansas. He was buried near his cabin in the garden.

His grave was dug by his wife and daughter who prepared puncheons of proper size and thickness to substitute for a coffin. The grave was not over two feet deep. There were many Shawnee present, and many items were deposited with the body. All seemed to be deeply affected.

After the burial of the old chief, the Shawnees slaughtered a beef, cooked and prepared the meat, and held a sort of feast. One of his surviving relatives was Little Fox who went to Kansas with the rest of the tribe.

Simon Girty

Simon Girty as he was called became leader of the band of Mingoes in Ohio. He was born on an island in the Susquehanna River in 1741. His father's name was also Simon, and his mother's maiden name was Crosby. The father was killed in a drunken frolic, leaving four sons: Thomas, James, George and Simon.

The widow subsequently married John Turner, and bore him one son, John. During the French war, the family members were captured, and the elder Turner was burned at the stake, and the balance of the family taken into captivity. Thomas escaped, James was adopted by the Shawnees, George by the Delawares, and Simon by the Senecas. To what tribe the mother and child, John Turner, were assigned is unknown.

Simon Girty married Catherine Malott who bore him five children: John who died in infancy, Ann, Thomas, Sarah and Predaux whose descendants are numerous. Simon Girty died near Amherstburg, Canada, February 18, 1818. During his life, he was described with dark, shaggy hair, low forehead, contracted brows, gray eyes and thin, compressed lips.

Ellskwatawa

Ellskwatawa, the triplet brother of Tecumseh, is known in history as the prophet. He is often referred to as the "One Eyed Prophet," from his being blind in one eye. The brother of Tecumseh was an orator of great renown, and a religious teacher.

During the first fifty years of his life from his birth in 1768, it was not remarkable. It was not until one day as he was lighting his pipe, he fell backward in his cabin, upon his bed, and continued for sometime lifeless, to all appearances. Preparations were made for his interment, and it was not until the tribe was assembled, as usual for such occasions, and they were in the act of removing him, that he revived.

His first words were, "Don't be alarmed. I have seen heaven. Call the nation together, that I may tell them what has appeared to me." When they were assembled, he told them that two beautiful young men had been sent from heaven by the Great Spirit, who spoke thus to him:

"The Great Spirit is angry with you, and will destroy all the red men unless you refrain from drunkeness, lying and stealing, and turn yourselves to him, you shall never enter the beautiful place which we will show you."

He was then conducted to the gates of heaven, from whence he could behold all its beauties, but was not permitted to enter. After undergoing hours' tantalization, from extreme desire of participating in its indescribable joys and pleasures, he was dismissed. His conductors told him to tell all the tribes what he had seen, to repent of their ways, and they would visit him again.

This story varies.

At an early age he did disappear from his relatives, and was considered to be lost. That he strolled to Quebec, and from thence to Montreal, where he engaged to pilot a vessel to Halifax, at which point he remained for several years, and in this period of time, received an education that enabled him to act the part of prophet and medicine man.

In his intercourse with the British, he no doubt learned that a comet would appear in the year 1811, -- a fact that he and Tecumseh used with considerable effect in their prophecies.

After five years of continuous effort, the Prophet assisted by Tecumseh collected a thousand warriors gathered from the Shawnees, Delawares, Wyandots, Potawatomis, Ottawas, Kickapoos, Chippewas and others, and located themselves on territory that had previously been ceded to the United States.

Tecumseh and the Prophet sent messages to General Harrison, in which they asserted that the territory ceded to the United States at the treaty of Fort Wayne, was made by irresponsible parties -- that the chiefs who negotiaged the treaty had no authority to cede the lands of the nations.

Tecumseh and the Prophet finally visited General Harrison at Vincennes to make known their grievances. The General received them and consented to discuss the questions at issue. The Prophet, however, instead of proceeding at once to set forth his complaints, indulged in many singular antics of conjuring the general, after which strange exhibition, he paused and made an imperious demand that the United States surrender the lands which had been ceded by treaty with the several separate tribes. At the conclusion of the Prophet's harangue, Tecumseh delivered his celebrated speech.

The alternative being war, General Harrison accepted the challenge and the council broke up with both parties resolved upon hostilities. Tecumseh departed to enlist the nations of the South, and the Prophet betook himself to Tippecanoe to hold the disputed territory until his brother should return.

While Tecumseh was in the South, the tribal aggressions still continuing, General Harrison decided to penetrate to the Prophet's town and bring about some adjustment of existing difficulties. Accordingly, on the 6th of November 1811, he encamped with a force of 900 men, within a mile of the Prophet's headquarters. At four o'clock the next morning, the tribe attacked the American force, in which they suffered a signal defeat.

The defeated tribe was greatly exasperated with the Prophet, and reproached him in bitter terms for the calamity he had brought upon them, and accused him of the murder of their friends who had fallen in the action.

It seems, that after pronouncing some incantations over a certain composition which he had prepared on the night preceeding the action, he assured his followers, that, by the power of his art, half of the invading army was already dead, and the other half in a state of distraction. That the tribe would have little to do but rush into their camp and complete the work of destruction with their tomahawks.

"You are a liar," said one of the surviving Winnebagoes to him after the action, "for you told us the white people were dead, or crazy, when they were all in their senses, and fought like the devil."

The Prophet appeared dejected, and sought to excuse himself on the plea that the virtue of his composition had been lost by a circumstance of which he had no knowledge until after the battle. His sacred character was so far forfeited that the tribe bound him with cords and threatened to put him to death.

What really happened to him after the War of 1812 has been a question of dispute. Some say he went to Canada until he was exiled from there and others say that he remained in Ohio at Wapakoneta. He went west of the Mississippi with a large number of his tribe in 1828, and died of cholera in 1833 in Kansas.

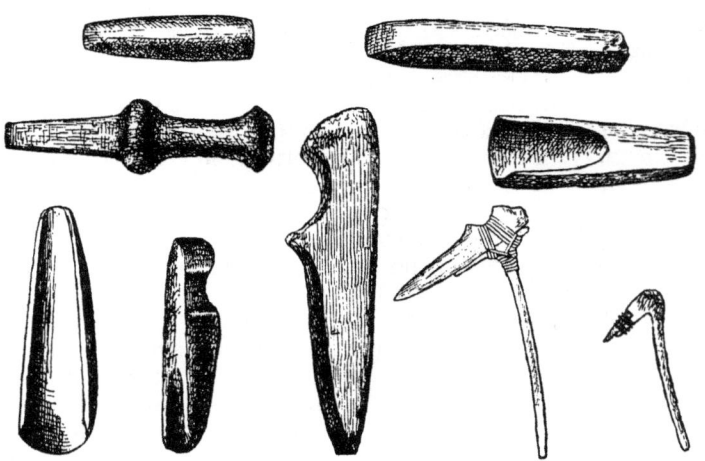

CHISELS, GOUGES AND ADZES.

THE WORLD OF THE GREAT SPIRIT
CHAPTER TWELVE

Most all tribes who settled in the state of Ohio believed in one Supreme Being. The Iroquois called him Hawenneyu while among the others he was known as Gicelamu-Kaong by the Delawares. They also believed in an evil spirit who was much like the devil in the Christian religion.

The Great Spirit was credited with the creation of man and all useful animals and products of the earth, but the Evil Spirit was supposed to have created all monsters, poisonous reptiles, and toxic plants. The Great Spirit made good for man while the Evil Spirit made bad for man.

All of the tribes made sacrifices and offerings to various spirits for favors such as rain for their crops, good weather, and the expulsion of evil spirits from men and women who were sick or who had committed a wrongdoing, or who were suspected of witchcraft. The only time they burned tobacco was when they were asking for favors from the Great Spirit believing that the smoke would carry their prayers to Him.

There were usually six regular festivals or thanksgivings. The first was the Maple Festival, then the Planting Festival, the Strawberry Festival, Green Corn Festival, Harvest Thanksgiving and the New Year's Festival.

All festivals began with speeches by the leaders throughout the day where everyone would gather to listen. Following the speeches was usually a dance which was considered a form of worship.

Heno or Hinun, the great Thunderer, was usually addressed if there was a drought and rain was needed for the crops. Thunderer was the guardian of the sky and was protrayed as a powerful brave armed with a bow and arrows of fire. His wife was Rainbow and his human aid was Gunnodoyak, a young warrior who fought the serpent of the Great Lakes.

After the special council was opened with speeches, the Ahdoweh were introduced which were short speeches given by various individuals who gave thanks to others and things. The appointed leader as "Keeper of the Faith" would make the main invocation.

The Delawares also believed that the Great Spirit or

GicelamuKaong was assisted by four powerful manitous or gods of the four cardinal directions.

Another name for the Great Spirit was Kici Manitou who had an assistant known as Nanabosho whose first gift to mankind was the Mide, a sacred ceremony arising out of the rivalry of the birth of quadruplets. Nanabosho was the eldest but the last, the fourth, killed the mother as it was born. In retaliation, Nanabosho eliminated the fourth child.

Kici Manitou wandered about in search of the place where the earth would arise. A tortoise told him where soil could be found and water birds brought it to him in their beaks. From this Kici Manitou then formed the earth and dried it in his sacred pipe.

Another name for the Great Spirit was Hahgwehdiyu who created goodness and light, the opposite of his brother Hahgwehdaetgah, the creator of evil. Haghwehdiyu created the world by making the outstretched palm the sky, the head of his dead mother, Ataensic, the sun, and her breasts the moon and stars. By making her body the earth, he turned her from a sky goddess into an earth mother. To counter this creation, Hahgwehdaetgah sent hurricanes and earthquakes and created darkness but he was defeated in a duel with his brother and banished to the underworld.

One of the legendary sages of the early Iroquois was Hiawatha who was an Onondaga chief who founded the League of the Five Nations also known as the Iroquois Confederacy in the 1500's. Hiawatha offered peace to all tribal peoples who would join together to maintain it. To others he offered this invitation: "And you of the different nations of the south, and you of the west may place yourselves under our protection, and we will protect you. We earnestly desire the alliance and friendship of you all."

A powerful shaman or medicine man Atotarho opposed the league's formation and killed Hiawatha's wife and daughter. The man was extremely tormented over the situation until leaders prayed for him and restored him to normal. That is, Atotarho was restored to normal. He and Hiawatha were reconciled thus uniting the five different tribes into the league -- the Cayuga, the Mohawk, the Oneida, the Onondaga and the Seneca.

The peaceful alliance welcomed others into its fold. The peace unity lasted longer than any other confederacy. The tribes themselves understood the nature of their League and sang at their council fires:

"I come again to greet and thank the League;
I come again to greet and thank the kindred;

I come again to greet and thank the warriors;
I come again to greet and thank the women.
My forefathers, -- what they established --
My forefathers, -- hearken to them!
Hail, my grandsires!"

    Another famous dueling pair of brothers were Iouskeha who was inclined to good while his brother Tawiscaron preferred evil things. They fought a bloody fight for supremacy, which Iouskeha narrowly won. Thereafter, Tawiscaron was obliged to keep his bad actions within bounds.
    Other names for the evil and good brothers were Glooskap and Malsum. Malsum killed his mother by forcing himself out of her armpit. He then created everything which he thought would inconvenience mankind, and made repeated attempts to kill his brother.
    However, Glooskap killed Malsum with the only weapon that could end his charmed life, the root of a fern. Malsum thereafter lived in the underworld as a wolf, while Glooskap protected mankind from evil monsters and natural forces.

Pontiac, a legendary Ottawa chief in the 1760's, tried to unite the different tribes living near the Great Lakes in an alliance against the encroachment of the European settlers. In order to gain support for this alliance, he told a story about a Delaware brave who had dreamed of meeting the sky god on a beautiful mountain.

"Red-coated men have come to trouble your lands," the deity said. "Drive them away. Wage war against them. Send them back to the lands I have made for them."

Pontiac's dream of alliance was ended when he was assassinated.

Winpe, a terrible sorcerer and an opponent of Glooskap, stole Glooskap's family and carried them off in a canoe. However, Glooskap pursued him on the back of a great fish and overcame his magic. The sorcerer fell dead to the ground, like a mighty pine tree.

Dreams, stories and fantasies were created to achieve results. Most of the philosophies promoted by the tribes were geniunely good toward all peoples.

Hiawatha said it all when he stated:

"We must unite ourselves into one common band of brothers. We must have but one voice. Many voices makes confusion. We must have one fire, one pipe, and one war club. This will give us strength."

This unity was achieved through family of common language, common origins, common values and fellow-feeling. Among the tribes, it was the principle of majority rule that was unthinkable. For though the League constituted a state, it was a special kind of state, built on and by means of bonds of kinship.

ANTECDOTES AND OTHER STORIES
CHAPTER THIRTEEN

Judge Elliott and the Indians

Toward the end of the 19th century, an adventurous young Pennsylvanian located himself as an Indian trader on the point of high land that juts out into the first bottom of the Licking Valley, known as Montour's Point, and upon which stands the mansion of Charles Montgomery, four miles East of Newark, near the Bowling Green Run, and also in sight of where afterwards individuals known as Hughes and Ratliff built their cabins. Montour's Point was named in honor of the Seneca, Andrew Montour, who was the companion of Christopher Gist in his western travels of 1751.

Here, Elliott, the trader, had temporarily established himself in a small hut or wigwam for money-making purposes, as a dealer in such goods as he might be able to trade to the tribe of the village adjoining.

Elliott prospered for a time, but one day a friendly tribal woman informed him of a plot to take his scalp and appropriate his effects. He took in the situation at a glance, and with commendable haste, gathered together his valuables and secretly mounted his horse and left on the most direct trail to the east side of the Ohio River.

The braves were in hot pursuit of him, nearly the entire distance, and he barely escaped with his life. The braves confiscated his goods he left behind but they never got his scalp.

Memoir of Daniel Carter

My father settled in the wilderness one mile northeast of where Ashland now is on February 12, 1812. I was then between nine and ten years of age being born May 23, 1802 just the age for such events as then occurred to make a deep and lasting impression on my memory.

That spring Benjamin Cuppy, Jacob Fry, Mrs. Sage and family and Stephen Trickel moved into the neighborhood, all built cabins, cleared land, planted corn and potatoes and all went well for some time.

The tribes were living at their villages, Jerometown and Greentown and came frequently to our house. Sometimes there were forty or fifty of them at a time, but they were always peaceable and friendly. Father and mother always tried to treat them kindly; fed them when they came hungry, lodged them as best as they could, which had its effect when they made their raid on the frontiers.

The British were trying to influence all the tribes of Indians to join them and fight the Americans. A chief of some tribe visited Chief Pipe at Jerometown and Armstrong, the chief of Greentown, and used his best endeavors to persuade them to join the British in the war against America. The Indians agreed to call a council and decide on the course they would pursue. The council was held and they decided to remain neutral. I was sent to Odell's mill with a sack of corn and had to go through Jerometown as there was no other trail.

When I returned in the evening, they were holding their war dance. They wanted me to stay and see the performance. I hitched my horse and staid till the dance was over, then rode home, a distance of nine miles through the wilderness, arriving at home about two o'clock in the morning.

This chief visited all the states and territories. Where he could get their consent to join the British, he would give them a red stick in token of blood. Consequently he was known as the chief red-stick. This council at Jerometown was held about the last of June 1812. But after Hull's surrender August 16, 1812, the government thought best to remove them; not so much for fear of their making trouble, but to keep them from harboring unfriendly Indians.

When Captain Douglas informed them that he came with orders to remove them, they were much excited and would not consent to go. Captain Douglas called on Mr. Copus to go with him and use his influence to obtain their consent. Mr. Copus replied that he and the tribe were on friendly terms and they would not think it kind in him to persuade them to leave against their wills. But Douglas threatened to arrest him as a traitor if he refused.

As they could not talk with them, Mr. Copus was prevailed upon to go as an interpreter. He told them that they would consent to go their property should be taken care of and that the officer had authorized him to say so, on the strength of this promise they reluctantly consented to go. They packed up what they could take with them and started. They had not gone more than two miles when looking back, they saw their village on fire, some of Douglas' soldiers having lingered behind and applied the fatal torch.

....As I had frequently seen Captain Pipe, chief of the Jerometown Indians, perhaps it would not be amiss to give a short description of him. He was about six feet in height, straight and well proportioned, rather round features, slightly pale face with a grave countenance and to appearance was about fifty years of age and I should judge had perhaps one-fourth white blood in his veins.

I have also seen Armstrong, the chief of the Greentown Indians, and think he had a mixture of white blood in him. I will give the location of those towns for the satisfaction of those who were not here until the last traces of them were wiped out.

Jerometown was situated one and one-fourth miles a little southwest from Jeromeville, on the state road from Wooster to Mansfield. Greentown was in the Black Fork valley about five miles southeast of Petersburg.

I saw Captain Lyon, one of the Jerometown Indians shortly after the war was over. He knew me and asked if we had seen them when they went up to burn Cuppy and Fry's houses. I answered "no." He then asked if we had seen their tracks in the corn field? I replied, "yes." He then said, "we saw you and would have gone to the house and got something to eat but we were afraid you would be frightened; we did not wish to scare you."

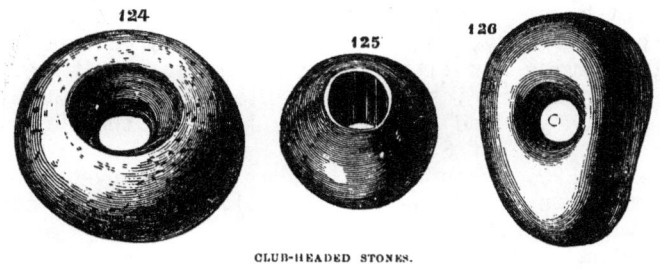

CLUB-HEADED STONES.

Katotawa

Old Katotawa was a chief of one of the many tribes of Indians of later Ashland County. Through a valley runs a small stream which has its course near Polk and flows southward, unites with the creeks east of Ashland and flows into what is called Jeromefork.

On the banks of the former stream, Old Katotawa or Chatachtawaugh often pitched his tent and fished its waters which are always cool being fed by fresh water springs and small tributaries, and once well stocked with river trout. When advancing civilization reached this point, the tribes were moving toward the setting sun.

Katotawa, then a very old man, remained alone in his hut on the banks of the stream, the few remaining days of his life. Some say that he was killed -- beheaded; and the superstitious claimed that his ghost -- the ghost of a headless body wandered along the river on dark and foggy nights.

The stream has ever since been known by that name which was given by this old sachem.

Johnnycake and his Wife

Johnnycake was well known to the early settlers. He was a tall, well built, fine looking man, of genial temper, good moral habits and enjoyed much the society of his friends.

His wife was a half-Delaware -- the daughter of an American woman who had been taken prisoner by the Indians, near Pittsburg, Pennsylvania. Her mother, after several years of captivity, made her escape, and returned to her family, leaving her little daughter among the tribe.

Johnnycake first lived in Clear Creek township of Ashland County, and in 1824, he lived in the vicinity of the present site of Savannah.

In 1829, when the Delawares were removed to their new home, west of the Mississippi, Johnnycake and his family went along.

Johnnycake died on the Delaware reservation in Kansas, leaving two or three sons. In the war of the Rebellion of 1861-5, three grandsons of Johnnycake served in Company M, 6th Regiment of Kansas Volunteer Infantry, under Captain John W. Duff. Their names were: John, Benjamin and Philip Johnnycake.

EARLY BLOCKHOUSES OR FORTIFIED STATIONS AND INCIDENTS
CHAPTER FOURTEEN

Blockhouses or fortified stations were destined to play an active part in the Indian and pioneer affairs of the Symmes Purchase and in many other parts of Ohio.

A strong log blockhouse being put up, it was surrounded by the cabins of the settlers, rather closely crowded together, and the whole was then encircled by a stout stockade or picket, made of tree trunks or legs set pretty deep in the ground, and making, in some cases, a really formidable work of defence.

A single county would have many stations as the population of the county or territory required. For example in Hamilton County which was situated between the Great and Little Miami Rivers, there were several such stations.

Covalt's Station, at Round Bottom, twelve miles up the Little Miami, below the present site of Milford, was erected in 1789. Abraham Covalt began the station and at least 20 soldiers from Fort Washington were garrisoned there. Unfortunately Covalt was killed by the Indians as given in a contemporary account by Thomas Fitzwater and William Fitzwater.

Towards noon on the first day in which Buckingham, Fletcher and Covalt started on their hunt, Covalt began to get very uneasy and to urge the others to return home, saying, there might be Indians about. The other two told him there was no danger, but this did not satisfy him. The nearer night approached the more importunate he became, and the more he urged them to return. This uneasiness in Covalt's mind, Buckingham always viewed as a bad omen. His entreaties finally prevailed on the others and they consented to return. So they felt the "licks" in order to reach the station while it was yet daylight.

Arriving opposite to where Buckingham's mill now stands, while Covalt and Fletcher were walking close together, and Buckingham about three rods behind, suddenly three guns were fired about twenty yards distant. Buckingham looked forward and saw Covalt and Fletcher start to run down the Miami, and also saw three Indians jump over a log, yelling and screaming like demons. As Buckingham wheeled to run up the river, he tried to throw off his blanket, but it hung over his shoulders like a powderhorn, as the strap passed over his head. When he did get it loose, it took his hat with it. He ran up but a few poles, then took up the hill, the river and hill being close together. As he went up the hill, he looked back several times, but saw no one in pursuit. When he arrived on the top, he got his gun ready for emergency, then stopped, looked back, and listened. While thus standing, he heard the Indians raise the yell down in the bottom, thirty or forty rods distant, then he knew they had caught one or both of the others. When he found the Indians were that distance from him, he knew that he could make tracks as fast as they could follow him. So he steered over the hills and came to the Miami, at what is now Quail's railroad bridge. Getting to the station, he found that Fletcher had got there a few minutes before him. By this time it was night.

Fletcher's story of the affair was that he and Covalt ran together some distance, when Fletcher's feet became entangled in a grapevine, and down he fell, where he laid perfectly still until the Indians passed him. One passed close to him, no doubt thinking he had fallen to rise no more. And they all kept on in hot pursuit of Covalt. As soon as they got of sight, Fletcher made his escape down the river. Next morning, a party of men left the station to look for Covalt. Arrived at the place, they found his body, his scalp, gun, tomahawk, powderhorn, blanket, knife, hat, and part of his clothes gone, and an old broken rifle near his body. The Indian traces showed that they had crossed and re-crossed at Indian Ripple. They were not traced any farther.

Dunlap's Station was established in the early spring of 1790 in Colerain township on the east side of the Great Miami and in the remarkable bend of that stream which begins about a half mile south of the county line.

The station was begun by John Dunlap, an Irishman from Colerain, in the north of Ireland. Several settlers built their cabins there around the station. In early January 1791, Indians attacked the settlement. The story of the seige was recorded in McBride's Pioneer Biography.

Before sunrise on the morning of the tenth of January, just as the women were milking the cows in the fort, the Indians made their appearance before it, and fired a volley, wounding a soldier named McVicker. Every man in the fort was immediately posted to the best advantage by the commander, and the fire returned. A parley was then held at the request of the Indians, and Abner Hunt, whom

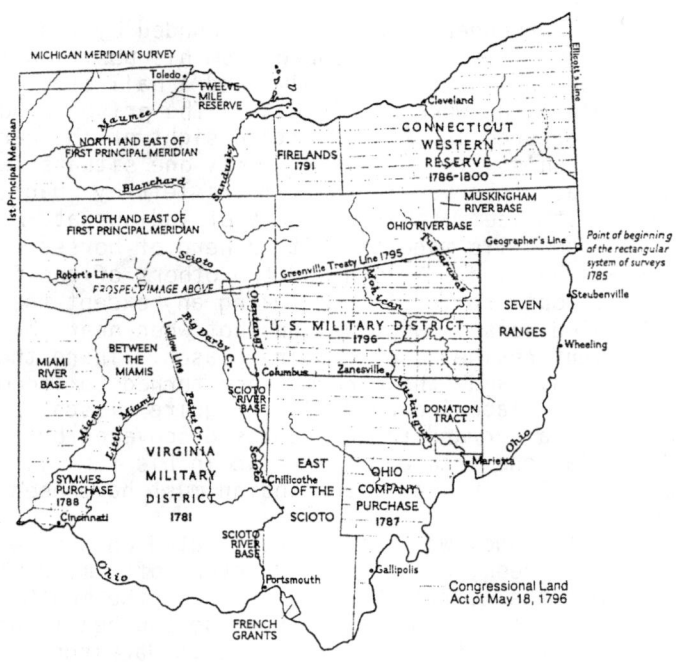

they had taken prisoner as before mentioned, was brought forward securely bound, with his arms pinioned behind him, by an Indian, or as some say, the notorious Simon Girty, the leader of the party, holding him by the rope. Mounting him on a stump within speaking distance of the garrison, he was compelled to demand and urge the surrender of the place, in the hope of saving his own life, he did in the most pressing terms, promising that if it were done, life and property would be held sacred. Not a single individual in the fort, however, would agree to a surrender. Lieutenant Kingsbury took an elevated position where he could overlook the pickets, and promptly rejected all their propositions, telling them that he had dispatched a messenger to Judge Symmes, who would soon be up to their relief, with the whole settlement on the Ohio. He failed, however, to impose on them. They replied it was a lie, as they knew Judge Symmes was then in New Jersey, and informed him they had five hundred warriors, and would soon be joined by three hundred more, and that, if an immediate surrender was not made, they would all be massacred, and the station burned. Lieutenant Kingsbury replied that he would not surrender if he were surrounded by ten thousand devils, and immediately leaped from his position into the fort. The Indians fired at him, and a ball struck off the white plume he wore on his hat. The prisoner Hunt was cruelly tortured and killed within sight of the garrison.

Nelson's Station was an early one situated west of Madison as preserved in the memoirs left by Daniel Hosbrook. It seems that a party of Indians at one time toward the hills made off with a herd of horses, one of which was hoppled. Nelson and the others of the fort made pursuit, but failed in overtaking any except the one on the hoppled horse, whom Nelson shot when near the site of the present residence of Esquire Clason. There the Indian was buried, and the circumstance turned to account by naming the place Indian Hill. Esquire Clason says that many years afterward the grave was discovered by accident, and the jawbone secured as a relic in his family. Judging from the relic, he says, the Indian must have been a giant in proportion.

Fort Finney was said to be located on the west bank of a small creek, about three-quarters of a mile above the mouth of the Little Miami, and near the mouth of the creek, not far from what is now the southeast corner of the former farm of the late John Scott Harrison.

A early narrative was preserved by John Scott Harrison when he addressed the Whitewater and Miami Valley Pioneer Association in 1866.

A party of men residing at the Point (mouth of the Big Miami) were returning from a small mill near the North Bend, and with one exception, stopped at the old log house lately occupied by Andrew McDonald, where a tavern was then kept; and as this was before the days of temperance societies, it is a very fair inference that they stopped to take a drink. One man, Demoss, more temperate, perhaps, then his fellows, continued on his way up the hill -- the trace to the Point then running over the hill, near the old graveyard, and on the bluff of the ridge. The revelers had hardly time to accomplish the object of their stop before the report of a rifle was heard on the hill. The party at the tavern, supposing it was only an intimation from their more sober companion to cease their revels and continue their way home, rushed out of the house with a wild whoop, mounted their horses, and rode up the hill. But what must have been the horror of the party, on arriving at the crown of the hill, to find their companion dead and weltering in his blood. The undischarged rifle of Demoss, and the missing mealbag, too plainly explained the manner and cause of his death. Pursuit was immediately given, in a northwesterly direction, and the meal, but not the Indian, found. The Indian, in order to save his own life, had dropped that which had evidently incited him to commit the murder.

Pleasant Valley Station was on the line between sections four and ten, Springfield township, near the Station Spring. It was built in 1794 by the builders of Tucker's Station, to protect them and another party which had moved in to the westward.

According to a historian by the name of Olden, neither Tucker's nor Pleasant Valley stations suffered any serious trouble with the Indians. No murders or other depredations were committed, and, save one single incident, nothing occurred to cause alarm or apprehension of danger. The event referred to happened one morning during the witner of 1793-94. Mr. James Seward, while down at the spring getting water, heard what he supposed to be turkeys calling some distance beyond the creek, and on going into the station-house spoke to a Mr. Mahan, who had been about the station several days, saying: "If you would like to have a turkey, Mahan, I think you can get one if you hurry out. I heard them calling over on the hill." Mahan at once caught up his gun and started in the direction pointed out by Seward. He had gone but a short distance when he heard the peculiar calling of turkeys, and followed on in the direction until he was led away near a mile from the station, when suddenly a large Indian stepped from behind a tree not more than twenty yards from him, and said in broken English, "How do?" At the same time he saw a gun pointing towards him from a cluster of spice bushes. The surprise was so great and sudden that he dropped his gun and ran with superhuman speed for the station, followed closely by the Indians. They no doubt intended capturing him without alarming the settlement, and therefore did not fire upon and kill him at once, as they could easily have done....He outstripped his pursuers and reached the station, but so overcome that his eyes were protruding and bloodshot. He swooned from exhaustion, and lay for an hour or more in a complete stupor. When reaction came a fever set in, and for several days his life was despaired of.

White's Station was formed under the leadership of Captain Jacob White of Redstone, Pennsylvania, by a number of families, among the heads of whom were Messrs. David Flinn, Andrew and Moses Pryor, Andrew Goble and Lewis Winans. The exact date is unknown. Local traditions fix the year as 1790; but as Captain White did not locate his land until July 23, 1792, it believed that he did not go upon it with his settlement until after that date. It was at this station the families had a great deal of trouble with the local tribes in the area.

Griffin's Station was about half a mile west of White's and was probably established in the fall of 1793, or soon afterwards. Lieutenant Daniel Griffin, upon a land warrant, July 23, 1792, entered the entire section seven, now in this township, and some time after sold three and forty-eight acres of it to James Caldwell.

Voorhee's Station was located upon section 33 near the present towns of Lockland and Reading. It was not a block-house, or even stockade, but a large, strong log cabin, which answered for both residence and defence, and was frequently mentioned in the early times, in speech and print, as Voorhee's Station.

An early incident in the area was reported in the autumn of 1794 with a William Moore who made his home at Covalt's Station. While out on one of his hunting expeditions, he wandered to the Great Lick as it was then called and east of White's Station. He there killed a deer, which he skinned, and had prepared the saddle for packing, and while in the act of washing his hands in the brook, and at the same time amusing himself by singing an Indian song he had learned while a captive among the Shawnees, he was suddenly alarmed by a voice joining in the song in the Indian tongue. He instantly sprang to his feet and ran for the thick wood on the west, closely pursued by some Indians. He made to White's Station, with the loss of his gun and coat, and also his game.

BIBLIOGRAPHY OF SOURCES CONSULTED

Andrews, Ralph W. INDIAN LEADERS WHO HELPED SHAPE AMERICA. Seattle, WA: Superior Publishing Co., 1971.
Atwater, Caleb. DESCRIPTION OF THE ANTIQUITIES OF THE STATE OF OHIO & OTHER WESTERN STATES. Ohio: American Antiquarian Society for State of Ohio, 1820.
Baughman, A. J., editor. HISTORY OF ASHLAND COUNTY, OHIO. Chicago: S.J. Clarke Publishing Company, 1909.
Bryan, Chester E., editor. HISTORY OF MADISON COUNTY, OHIO. Chicago: Beers Publishing Co., 1905.
Caldwell, J.A., editor. HISTORY OF BELMONT & JEFFERSON COUNTIES, OHIO. Wheeling, WVA: Historical Publishing Co., 1880.
Campbell, Rev. T.J. PIONEER LAYMAN OF NORTH AMERICA. New York: The America Press, 1916.
Cotterell, Arthur. THE MACMILLAN ILLUSTRATED ENCYCLOPEDIA OF MYTHS AND LEGENDS. New York: Macmillan Pub. Co., 1989.
Cranz, David. ANCIENT AND MODERN HISTORY OF THE BRETHREN. London: W & A Strahan, 1780.
Dills, R.S., editor. HISTORY OF GREENE COUNTY, OHIO. Dayton, Ohio: Odeli & Maver Pub., 1881.
Graham, A.A., editor. HISTORY OF FAIRFIELD & PERRY COUNTIES, OHIO. Chicago: W.H. Beers & Co., 1883.
Graham, A.A., editor. HISTORY OF RICHLAND COUNTY, OHIO. Mansfield, Ohio: A.A. Graham & Co., Pub., 1880.
Griswold, Bert J., editor. FORT WAYNE, GATEWAY TO THE WEST, 1802-1813. Indianpolis: Historic Bureau of Indiana Library & History Dept., 1927.
Heckewelder, John. NARRATIVE OF THE MISSION OF THE UNITED BRETHREN. Philadelphia: McCarty & Davis, 1820.
Heisey, John W. "Who Was Indian Kate?" TRI-STATE TRADER. Knightstown, Ind.: November 1987.
Hildreth, Samuel P., M.D. EARLY HISTORY OF THE NORTHWEST INCLUDING MORAVIAN MISSIONS IN OHIO. Cincinnati: Hitchcock & Walden, 1864.
HISTORY OF ALLEN COUNTY, OHIO. Chicago: Warner, Beers & Co., 1885.
HISTORY OF BROWN COUNTY, OHIO. Chicago: W.H. Beers & Co., 1883.

HISTORY OF CLARK COUNTY, OHIO. Chicago: W.H. Beers & Co., 1881.
HISTORY OF CLERMONT COUNTY, OHIO. Philadelphia: Louis H. Everts, 1880.
HISTORY OF CLINTON COUNTY, OHIO. Chicago: W.H.Beers & Co., 1882.
HISTORY OF DELAWARE COUNTY, OHIO. Chicago: O.L. Baskin & Co. Historical Pub., 1880.
HISTORY OF LORAIN COUNTY, OHIO. Philadelphia: Williams Bros., 1879.
HISTORY OF MONTGOMERY COUNTY, OHIO. Chicago: W.H. Beers & Co., 1882.
HISTORY OF ROSS & HIGHLAND COUNTIES, OHIO. Cleveland, Ohio: W.W. Williams, Printers, 1880.
HISTORY OF TRUMBULL & MAHONING COUNTIES, OHIO. Cleveland: H.Z. Williams & Bro., 1882.
Hodge, Frederick Webb. HANDBOOK OF AMERICAN INDIANS NORTH OF MEXICO. Two parts. Washington,D.C.: Government Printing Office, 1907.
Hopley, John E., editor. HISTORY OF CRAWFORD COUNTY, OHIO. Chicago: Richmond-Arnold Pub. Co., 1912.
Kappler, Charles J. INDIAN AFFAIRS: LAWS & TREATIES. VOLUME II. Washington, D.C.: Government Printing Office, 1904. [Author's note: Individual Native American and Native American Related Names were taken from this version of the treaties.]
Lossing, Benson J. THE PICTORIAL FIELD-BOOK OF THE WAR OF 1812. New York: Harper & Bros. Pub., 1868.
Mereness, Newton D. TRAVELS IN AMERICAN COLONIES. New York: Macmillan Co., 1916.
Miles, Walter K. "Tracing Indian Ancestry Challenging." TRI-STATE TRADER. Knightstown, Ind. 24 April 1982.
National Archives. AMERICAN INDIANS: A SELECT CATALOG OF MICROFILM PUBLICATIONS. Washington, D.C.: National Archives Trust Fund Board, 1984.
PORTRAIT & BIOGRAPHICAL RECORD OF GUERNSEY COUNTY, OHIO. Chicago: C.O. Owen & Co., 1895.
Rice, Rev. William H. DAVID ZEISBERGER & HIS BROWN BRETHREN. Bethlehem, PA: Moravian Pub. Concern, 1908.
Sheppard, Sally. INDIANS OF THE EASTERN WOODLANDS. New York-London: Franklin Watts Inc., 1975.
Smucker, Isaac. CENTENNIAL HISTORY OF LICKING COUNTY, OHIO. Newark, Ohio: Clark & Underwood Prters, 1876.

Sutton, Felix. NORTH AMERICAN INDIANS. New York: Wonder Books, 1965.
Smithsonian Institution. TEACHER'S RESOURCE GUIDE. Washington, D.C.: Smithsonian, 1988.
Tregillis, Helen Cox. PRIMER FOR AMERICAN INDIAN ANCESTRY SEARCHING. Author, 1990.
Bureau of Indian Affairs. TRIBAL LEADERS DIRECTORY. Washington, D.C.: U.S. Dept. of the Interior, January 1992.
Thwaites, Reuben Gold, editor. THE JESUIT RELATIONS AND ALLIED DOCUMENTS. Several volumes. Cleveland: The Burrows Brothers, 1900.
Vlahos, Olivia. NEW WORLD BEGINNINGS: INDIAN CULTURES IN THE AMERICAS. Greenwich, Ct.: Fawett Pub. Co., 1972.
Webber, Joe D., editor. "Indian Cessions Within the Northwest Territory." ILLINOIS LIBRARIES. Springfield, Ill.: Vol. 61 No. 6. June 1979.
Williamson, C.W. HISTORY OF WESTERN OHIO AND AUGLAIZE COUNTY. Columbus, Ohio: Press of W.M. Linn & Sons, 1905.

INDEX

Note: Native American individuals with more than one name are cross-indexed. Pronounce each Native American name to identify a possible variant spelling thereof.

Acoolatha or Little Fox, 61
Adams County, 17
Adena Culture, i
Ageupeh, 46
Agusquenah, 50
Ahdoweh, 91
Akapee or Heap Up Anything, 45
Alawemetahuck or Lullaway or Perry, 45
Alder, Jonathon, 45
Alleghenies, 14
Allegheny River, 48
Algonquin, i,44,55,63
Allen County, 40,45
Amacunca or Little Beaver, 61
Ameghqua, 61
Amenahehan or Capt. Crow, 57
American Revolution, 48
Amherstburg, Canada, 87
Ancestry, 10
Anderson or Kithuwheland, 56,57
Animals, 9
Annapolis, 70
Annenraes, 26
Anondironnons, 48
Apacahund or White Eyes, 57
Aquashequa, 45
Arbe Croche, 63
Arkbuckle, Capt. 77
Armstrong or Pamoxet, 50,57,69,73,74,96,97
Armstrong, George, 39
Armstrong, James or Jeeshawau, 57
Armstrong, John or Mahawtoo, 39,57,74

Armstrong, Joseph, 57
Armstrong, Robert, 37
Armstrong, Silas or Sanoudoyourayquaw, 39,57
Armstrong, Thomas, 73,74
Armstrong, Widow or Tishatahoones, 57,74
Aronzon or Twilight, 61
Arrowheads, etc., 23,25
Artaishnaiwan, 65
Aruntue, T., 37
Ash, 50
Ashelukah, 45
Ashland, 95
Ashland County, 98
Ataensic, 92
Atchatchakengouen, 59
Athelwakesoca or Yellow Clouds, 45
Atlantic Coast, 55
Atotarho, 92
Aubaway, 65
Aughquamauda or Difficulty, 61
Auglaize River, 44,45,46, 77,79,81,83,84
Augooshaway, 63
Aumatourow, 38
Auonasechla or Civil Man, 44
Aushewhowole, 38
Awaybariskecaw, 45
Aweallesa or Whirlwind, 57
Awmeyeeray, 35
Ayenucere, 57
Axtaca, 50

Babies, 2,4
Baker, Davy or Peetah, 45
Baptista, 45

108

Bath, 69,70
Battise, John, 72
Battisetown, 72
Bears, 9,10
Bearskin, 39
Bearskin or Muckquiona, 65
Bear's paw, 63
Beaubien, Josette, 61
Beaver, 57
Beaver, Capt. or Punchhuck, 57
Beaver (Fort McIntosh), 69
Beaver, Ben, 57
Beaver County, PA, 34
Beaver Hat or Pappellelond, 57
Beaver River, 56
Bellefontaine, 86
Between the Logs, 37,38,74
Bigarms, 38
Big Bear or Lapaphnihe, 57
Big Belt, 50
Big Body or Metche Keteta, 61
Big Bowl or Mechimenduch, 65
Big Miami River, 59,66,70,102
Big Cat or Hengue Pushees, 56
Big Darby, 70
Big Ears or Toworordu, 38
Bigelow, Lucy, 74
Bigelow, Russell, 74
Big Snake or Shemenetoo, 44
Big Spring, 32
Big Turtle or Shekoghkell, 49,51
Black Chief or Skahomet, 35
Black Fork Valley, 97
Blackhoof's Spring, 71

Blackhoof or Cutthewekasaw, 42,44,45,71,72,76
Blackhoof Town, 71
Black King or Lemantanquis, 56
Black Racoon or Teorow, 57
Black River, 9
Black Wolf, 42
Blanchard's Fork, 65
Blockhouses, 99
Blue Eyes, 74
Blue Jacket or Weyapiersenwaw, 42,44,45,79,80
Bondie, Antoine, 61
Boone, Daniel, 66
Boonesboro, 66
Boston, 70
Bouquet, ----, 55,79
Bowling Green, 66,67,95
Boys, 2,3
Braddock, Gen., 71
Bright Horn or Wasawotah, 45
Bright Horn or Wathethewela, 75,76,77
British, 44,48,59,72,75,77,81,88,96
Brooke Co, VA, 35
Brown, Adam or Tahunehawettee, 35
Brown, John D., 39
Brownstown, MI, 40,44
Buck, 57
Buckingham, ----, 99
Buckongahelas or Shingess, 56,78,79
Buck Wheat, 57
Buffalo, Capt. or Kishkopekund, 57
Burials, 6
Burnt His Body or Youwautowtoyou, 50
Byaseka or Wolf, 44
Bysaw, 50

Caawaricho, 45
Cabayaw, 65
Cabins, 1,2

109

Cabma, 61
Cacalawa or End of the Tail, 45
Caghkoo, Capt., 57
Caldwell, James, 104
Calequa, 45
Camp Ball, 37
Canada, 32,81,90
Canandaigua Lake, 28
Canesadooharaie River, 9
Capawah, 45
Capes, 45
Carolinas, 41,71
Carp or Namepich, 63
Carrying the Basket, 50
Carrying the News or Rewanyeato, 50
Carryumanduetaugh, 38
Carter, Daniel, 95
Cass, Gen. Lewis, 44,84,86
Cassman, Samuel, 57
Cat, 57
Cat Bone, 50
Caugooshow or Clearing Up, 50
Caumecus, 50
Caunaytoma, 38
Cauwauay or Striking, 50
Cauyou, 38
Cayuga, 26,28,48,92
Chacod, 45
Chakalowah or Tail's End, 44
Chaouanons or Shawnees, 41
Charlevois, 26
Charley, 61
Charlo or Oschano, 65
Chatachtawaugh or Katotawa, 98
Chatham, Ont., 82

Cheahaska or Capt. Tommy, 45
Checauk, 65
Chegoimegon, 63
Chegonickska, 63
Chenoweth's Trace, 70
Chepocura, 45
Cherokee, 59,81
Cherokee Boy or Harrowenyou or Horonu, 35,37,39
Chickasaws, 81
Chief, 5,11
Chillicothe, 20,22,42,44
Chippewas, 32,35,40,47,54, 56,59,62,63,88
Chiyamik, 38
Chochkelake or Dam, 45
Choctaws, 81
Chowelaseca, 45
Chub, 74
Chucatuh, 45
Cincinnati, 71,84
Civil John or Mesomea or Methomea, 49,50
Civil Man or Auonasechla, 44
Clamatonockis, 57
Clan Totem, 10,11
Clark, Gen., 71,77,83
Clark, George J., 39
Clark, Peter D., 39
Clark County, 44,67
Clarke, Alex., 39
Clason, Esquire, 102
Clear Creek Twp., 98
Clearing Up or Caugooshow, 50
Clinton County, 22
Clouding Up, 50
Cocheco, 50
Cochkepoghtogh, 61
Coffee House, 49,50
Coindos, 50
Colerain Twp., 100
Columbus, 34,73
Conawwwwehow, 50
Coneseta, 50
Conestoga, 49

Conhowdatwaw, 50
Connodose, 50
Conundahaw, 50
Coon, John or Isatouque, 38
Coon, Lewis, 38
Coon Lake, 33
Coon Stick, 51
Copus, ----, 96
Corn, 11,12
Cornstalk or Nerupeneshequal, 42,44, 45,77,78
Cornstalk, Peter or Penitchthamtah, 45,77
Cornstalk's Town, 67
Couauka, 50
Couewash, 50
Council House, 5,6
Covalt, Abraham, 99, 100
Covalt's Station, 99,104
Coventry, 69,70
Cowhousted, 50
Cowista, 50
Crane or Tarhe, 35
Crane or Twaatwaa, 50,59
Crane, Widow of or Yourowquains, 38
Crawford, Col. Wm., 34,73
Crawford County, 32,39, 70
Crayfiste, 50
Crescent or Wemetche, 61
Croghansville, 35,37
Crooked Nose's Place, 67
Crops, 1,2,33
Crosby, ----, 87
Cross the Arms or Taushaushaurow, 50

Crow, Capt. or Amenahchan, 57
Crying Often or Isetaune, 50
Cudeetore, 38
Cumberland River, 41
Cumberland Valley, 71
Cumchaw of Blanchard's Fork, 65
Cumchaw of Wolf's Rapids, 65
Cuppy, ----, 97
Cuppy, Benjamin, 95
Cuqua, 38
Curetscetau, 50
Curoweyottell, 38
Cutthewekasaw or Blackhoof, 42,44,71,72
Cuueshohant or Harris, 51
Cuyahoga, 69
Cuyahoga Falls, 69,70
Cuyahoga River, 56
Cyahaga or Fisher, 50

Dam or Chochkelake, 45
Darby, 34
Darlington, PA, 34
Dasharows, 38
Dashoree, 38
Dasquoerunt, 49
Datoowawna, 38
Dashowrowramou or Drifting Sand, 50
Daughshuttayah, 35
Dauoreenu, 38
Dauquausay, 38
Daureehau, 38
Daushouteehawk, 38
Dautoresay, 38
Dautsaqua, 38
Dawatont or John Hicks or Dauatout, 39
Dawews, 38
Dawhowhouk, 38
Dawson, Jared S., 39
Dawweeshoe, 38
Dayton, 66,81
Deecalrautousay, 38

Defiance, 84
Delaware, 3,32,34,35,40,
  44,47,54,55,56,57,
  58,62,67,69,73,74,
  87,88,94,98
Delaware River, 55
Delaware Villages, 69,
  70
Demoss, ----, 102
Detroit, 33,62,75,84
Detroit Rive, 33,80
Devil's Hole, 48
Dick, Jacob, 57
Difficulty or Aughqua-
  mauda, 61
Dog or Tondawgonie,
  65
Dondee, William, 57
Doonstough or Hunch
  on His Fore-
  head, 50
Dootooau, 38
Douglas, Capt., 96
Dresden, 66
Dress, 4,5
Driver, Isaac, 39
Duchouquet, Francis,
  83,84
Douhouquet Cemetery,
  85
Duff, Capt. John W.,
  98
Dunlap's Station,
  100
Dunquad or Half King
  or Doanquod, 39
Dunmore, Lord Gov.,
  34,41,42
Dusharraw, 38
Dutch, 55
Duyewtale, 38

Eaton, 66
Eauvaince, 65
Eddy or Kawachewau,
  65
Edington, Jess, 35
Edington, Thomas, 35

Eel-River, 32,40,54,58,62,
  82
Egatacumshequa, 45
Ellinipsico, 42,77,78
Elliot, Judge, 95
Ellskwatawa or Laulewas-
  ikau or Prophet, 81,
  88,89,90
Elsquatawa, 44
End of the Tail or Cacalawa,
  45
English, 63
Epaunnee, 46
Eries, 26,27,28,29,30,31,33,
  48,49
Ethewacase, 45
Evans, Lewis, 70
Evil Spirit, 91

Fairfield, Canada, 57
Fairfield County, 66
Fallen Timbers, 71,79
Fallen Timbers or Pht, 87
Falling Tree or Peeththa, 45
Feasts, 7,8
Finley, Rev. James B., 74
Fish Creek, 69
Fisher or Cyahaga, 50
Fishing, 8
Fitzwater, Thomas, 99
Fitzwater, William 99
Five Nations, 28,33,55
Flat Belly or Papskeecha,
  61
Fletcher, ----, 99,100
Flinn, David, 103
Florida, 71
Folks, George, 34
Fort Amanda, 79
Fort Defiance, 75
Fort DuQuesne, 78
Fort Finney, 102
Fort Industry, 35,40,54,62
Fort Jefferson, 66
Fort Laurens, 34
Fort McIntosh, 35,54,56,62
Fort Meigs, 73
Fort Niagara, 48

Fort Washington, 99
Fort Wayne, 75,81,83
Fort Winchester, 75
Fox River, 59
Fox Widow or Isanow-
    towtouk, 38
Francis, 61
Frankfort, KY, 76
Franklin County, 70
Franklinton, 70
French, 4,33,48,55,
    59,63,84
French Villages, 67
Fry, ----, 97
Fry, Jacob, 95
Fur Trade, 8

Galloway, Maj. James,
    72
Gardner, ----, 86
Gardner, James B., 46
Garrett, Charles B.,
    39
Garrett, George, 39
Garrett, Joe Walker,
    39
Gausawaugh, 38
Gearoohee, 38
Genesee River, 26,28,48
Geneva, 27
Gentaienton, 31
Georgesville, 70
Gicelamu Kaong, 91,92
Gillwas, 50
Girls, 3
Girty, Ann, 87
Girty, George, 87
Girty, James, 87
Girty, John, 87
Girty, Predaux, 87
Girty, Sarah, 87
Girty, Simon, 87,101
Girty, Thomas, 87
Gist, Christopher, 95
Give It to Her or
    Syunout, 50
Giveriahes, 38
Glooskap, 93,94

Goble, Andrew, 103
Godfroy, Francois, 61
Godfroy, Louis, 61
Going Up the Hill or
    Thucatrouwah, 45
Good Hunter, Capt., 51
Gooyeamee, 38
Grand Blaze, 56
Great Auglaize River 65
Grand Glaize King or
    Tetabokshke, 56
Great Hare or Michabou, 63
Great Kanawha, 41
Great Lakes, 26,94
Great Lick, 104
Great Miami River, 80,99,
    100
Great Spirit, 6,88,91
Green, Charles, 67
Green, George, 67
Green, Thomas, 69
Green Bay, 63
Green Corn Festival, 91
Greene County, 72
Greentown, 6,69,74,95,96,
    97
Greenville, 35,40,42,44,54,
    55,56,58,61,62,63,66,
    80,81,84,86
Grenadier Squaw, 44
Grenadier Squawtown, 67
Grey Eyes, Dr., 39
Grey Eyes, Matthew, 39
Griffin, Lt. Daniel, 104
Griffin's Station, 104
Gulf of Mexico, 14
Gunnodoyak, 91
Gurge or Tecutio, 45

Hackley, Rebecca, 61
Haghkela, 45
Hahgooseekaw or Capt.
    Reed, 44
Hahgwehdaetgah, 92
Hahgwehdiyu, 92
Hairlip, 50
Hairy River, 67
Half King or Donquad, 34,37,
    39

Half King's Son or
    Haroenyou or
    Haroenyor, 35
Half Up the Hill, 50
Halifax, 88
Halkootu, 45
Hamanchagave, 50
Hamilton, 66
Hamilton, George, 69
Hamilton County, 99
Hammel, Peter, 84
Hams, Capt., 50
Hamyautuhaw, 50
Hard Hickory, 50,51
Hardin, Col., 76,79
Hardin County, 32,72
Harmar, ----, 77,79
Harris or Cuuesho-
    hant, 51
Harris, Capt., 49
Harrison, ----, 84
Harrison, Gen., 75, 76,89
Harrison, John Scott, 102
Harrowenyou or
    Cherokee Boy, 35
Harvest Festival, 91
Harvey, ----, 72
Harvey, Henry, 86
Hatocuino, 46
Hauautounasquas, 50
Haucauarout, 50
Haudaunwaugh, 35
Haudonwauays or
    Stripping the
    River, 50
Hauleeyeatausay, 38
Haunarawreudee, 38
Haurauoot, 38
Hawdoro or Matthews, 39
Hawdorowwatistie or
    Billy Montour, 57
Hawenneyu, 91
Hawkinpumiska, 56
Hawreewaucudee, 38
Hayanoise or Ebenezer
    Zane, 38

Haysville, 73
Heckewelder, ----, 78
Helltown, 69
Hendricks, Joshua or
    Tyaudusont, 50
Hengue Pushees or Big Cat, 56
Hennepin, Louis, 26
Heno or Hinun or Thunderer, 91
Henry, 50
Henry, Lt. Col. or Kelel-
    amand, 56
Hiawatha, 92, 94
Hicks, Francis A., 39
Hicks, John or Wottondt or
    Dauatout, 38,39
Hill, Isaac, 57
Hillnepewayatuska, 50
Hinun or Heno or Thunderer, 91
His Blanket Down or
    Tousonecta, 51
His Neck Down, 50
Hock-Hocking, 66
Hog Creek, 44,45,46,87
Hold the Sky or Ramuye, 50
Holding His Hand About o
    Tauhaugainstoany, 50
Hole's Creek, 10
Honeoye, 28
Honey Creek, 37
Hoocue, 38
Hoogaudoorow, 38
Hoogaurow or Mad Man, 50
Hoomanrow or John Ming, 57
Hoondeshotch, 38
Hoonorowyoutacob, 38
Hopewell Culture, i
Hosbrook, Daniel, 102
Hottomorrow, 38
House Fly or Maggot, 50
Houtooyemaugh, 38
Hover, Ezekiel, 46
Howcuquawdorow, 38
Howdautauyeao or King
    George, 50
Howe's Historic Collection, 33

Hownorowduro, 38
Hownotant, 50
Howoner, 35
Howyouway or
    Paddling, 50
Hughes, ----, 95
Hull's, ----, 96
Hunch on His Forehead or
    Doonstough, 50
Hunt, Abner, 100,102
Hunt, George, 61
Hunter, G. or Trowyoudoys, 50
Hunting, 8,9
Huron River, 32,39,
    69,74
Hurons or Wyandots,
    26,27,32,33,34,
    35,36,37,38,39,
    47,48,54,55,63,
    70
Hurricane Tom's Town, 67
Hutchequa, 50
Hwtooyou, 38
Hyanashraman or
    Knife in His
    Hand, 50

Indiana, 58,61,83
Indian Cross Creek, 75
Indian Hill, 102
Indian Ripple, 100
Indianapolis, 86
Interpreters, 10
Iouskeha, 93
Irahkasquaw, 38
Iroquois, 26,30,31,
    41,48,63,70,
    91,92
Isaac or Youronocay, 50
Isahownusay, 49
Isanowtowtouk or
    Fox Widow, 38
Isatouque or John
    Coon, 38

Isetaune or Crying Often, 50
Iseumetaugh or Picking Up
    a Club, 50
Ishoreameusuwat, 38
Ishuskeah, 38
Island or Youwaydauyea, 50
Isohauhasay or Tall Chief, 50
Isontraudee, 38
Ispomduare or Yellowbay, 50
Isuhowhayeato, 38
Iyonayotha or Joe, 35

Jacobs, 78
Jaques, Henry, 39
Jeeshawau or James Armstrong, 57
Jelloway, 69
Jerome, 74
Jerome, John Baptiste, 69
Jeromefork, 98
Jerometown, 95,96,97
Jeromeville, 69,74,97
Jesuit Relation, 48
Joe or Iyonayotha, 35
Johnny, Capt., 42,75
Johnny Cake, 57,98
Johnnycake, Benjamin, 98
Johnnycake, John, 98
Johnnycake, Philip, 98
Johnnycake, Solomon, 57
Johnston, Col., 71,75,76, 83
Johnston, John, 86
Johnstown, 67
Joseph, 50
Jo Smee or Tahowtoorains, 50
Joso or Joseph Parks, 46

Kalamazoo River, 59
Kanakhib, 46
Kanhawa, 81
Kansas, 46,57,77,83,86,87,
    90,98

Kansas River, 77
Kaska, 45
Kaskaskia, 32
Kaskaskias, 40,54, 58,62
Katotawa, 98
Kawachewan or Eddy, 65
Kayketchheka or Wm. Perry, 45
Kaysewaesekah, 44
Keeahah, 42
Keenoshameek, 63
Keenquatakqua or Long Hair, 61
Keeper of the Faith, 91
Kekiapilathy, 42
Kekusthe, 45
Kelelamand or Lt. Col Henry, 56
Kentucky, 66
Keosakunga, 61
Ketauga or Charley, 61
Ketchum, Capt., 57
Ketoawsa, 46
Ketuchepa, 46
Kewapea, 45
Kiahoot, 50
Kici Manitou, 92
Kickapoo, 32,40,54, 58,62,88
Kikthawenund or Anderson, 56,57
Kilatika, 59
Killbuck, Capt., 57
King Beaverstown, 66
King George or Howdautauyeao, 50
Kingsbury, Lt., 101
Kishopekund or Capt. Buffalo, 57
Kiskapocke, 42
Kithtuwheland or Anderson, 57
Knife in His Hand or Hyanashraman, 50

Knisely's Spring, 70
Koehenna, 61
Koitawaypie or Col. Lewis or Quatawape, 44
Kumskaukau or Rumskaka, 81
Kusha, 65
Kuwashewon, 65

Labadie, Peter, 61
Lafontame, Francois, 61
Lake Erie, 26,65
LaMalice, 63
Lake Michigan, 59
Lake Ontario, 27
Lame Hawk, 42
Lamotothe, 45
Lane, Martin, 46
Langlois, Peter, 61
Lapaphnihe or Big Bear, 57
Large Bones or Tarsduhatse, 50
Lathowaynoma, 45
Laughshena, 45
Laulewasikau or Ellskwatawa or Prophet, 81
Lawathska, 45
Lawatucheh or John Wolf, 83
Lawaytucheh or John Wolf, 45
Lawetcheto, 46
Lawnoetuchu or Billy Parks, 46
Lawrenceburgh, 86
League of Five Nations, 92
Leather Lips or Shateyyaronyah, 35,73
Lebanon, 86
Lecuseh, 46
Leek or Sinnecowacheckowe, 50
Leemutque, 50
LeGris or Nagohquagogh, 61
Lemantanquis or Black King, 56
Lenape, 55
Lewis, Col. or Koitawaypie or Quatawape, 44,45

Lewis, Mary, 45
Lewistown, 40,45,46,
    49,80
Licking County, 15,20,
    66,67
Licking Valley, 95
Lithopolis, 66
Little Fox, 87
Little Fox or
    Acoolatha, 61
Little Fox or
    Oreroimo, 46
Little Jack, 57
Little Miami, 41,42,
    66,70,99,102
Little Otter or
    Nekeik, 65
Little Sandusky
    River, 57
Little Turtle or
    Meshekunnogh-
    quoh, 61,79,82,
    83
Lockland, 104
Logan, 49
Logan, Capt. or
    Spamagelabe,
    44,45
Logan, Capt. or
    Tahgahjute,
    75,76
Logan, Col. Benj.,
    81
Logan, James, 75
Logtown, 78
London, 70
Long, Ethan A., 39
Long, Irwin P., 39
Long Hair or Keen-
    quatakqua, 50,61
Long Shanks or Way-
    theah, 44
Looking at Her or
    Towotoyoudo, 50
Loramie, 66
Loramie Creek, 71
Lullaway or Alawemet-
    ahuck or Perry,
    45

Lyon, Capt., 97
Lyons, Thomas, 57,69

McArthur, Duncan, 44,84
McBride's Pioneer Bio.,
    100
McCarty or Tusqugan, 65
M'Carty, Rev. J.W., 20
McCulloch, Elliot, 39
McCulloch, Samuel, 39
M'Culloch, Widow or
    Mawcasharrow, 38
M'Collock, Wm., 37
McDonald, Andrew, 102
McDongal, Geo. or Skapoawah,
    45
McIlvaine, John, 46
McLean, John, 39
McNabb, William, 65
McNair, David or Thacaska,
    45
McPherson, Henry H., 46
McPherson, James, 46
McVicker, ----, 100

Machiwetah, 63
Mackacheek, 66
Mackinaw, 63
Madison, 102
Madison County, 22,34,70
Mad Man or Hoogaurow, 50
Madonrawcays, 38
Mad River, 10,42,44,66,
    67,70,71,81,83
Madudara, 38
Magathu, 45
Maggot or House Fly, 50
Maghpiway or Red Feather,
    56
Mahan, ----, 103
Mahawtoo or John Arm-
    strong, 57
Mahican, 55
Mahoma, 38
Mahoning River, 56
Mahoning Valley, 55
Makatewekasha or Black
    Hoof, 44

Malott, Catharine, 87
Malsum, 93
Manitou, 6
Manocue, 35
Mansfield, 97
Maple Festival, 91
Maple Sugar, 12
Mark on His Hip, 50
Marriage Customs, 3
Mascoutens, 59
Massasaugas, 56
Massie's Creek, 44
Matokrawtouk, 38
Matsayeaayourie, 38
Matthews or Undauwau
    or Hawdoro, 38,39
Maudamu, 38
Maugaugon, 37
Maumee, 10
Maumee Rapids, 44
Maumee River, 59,65,
    75,79
Maurawskinquaws, 38
Maurunquaws, 38
Mautanawto, 38
Mawcasharrow or
    Widow M'Cullock,
    38
Mawdovdoo, 38
Mawskattaugh, 38
Maydounaytove, 38
Mayeatohot, 38
Maywealiupe, 45
Mechimenduch or
    Big Bowl, 65
Medicine Men, 6
Mee Meea, 59
Meetheetashe, 81
Memhisheka, 45
Men, 3,4
Mengakonkia, 59
Menonkue or Thomas,
    38
Mentauteeboore, 50
Mentoududu, 50
Mequachuke, 42,44
Mesaukee, 65
Meshekunnoghquoh
    or Little Turtle,
    61

Meshenoqua or Little
    Turtle, 61
Mesherawah, 45
Mesomea or Civil John, 49
Metche Keteta or Big Body,
    61
Methomea or Civil John,
    50
Metosma, 61
Mewithaquiu, 46
Meyers, ----, 73
Miaghqua or Noon, 61
Miami Clans, 59
Miami County, 44,67
Miamis, 10,32,40,41,54,58,
    59,60,61,62,82
Miamisburg, 20
Miami River, 8,45,54,56,
    62,65
Miami Town, 70
Miami Valley, 10,71,72
Michabou or Great Hare,
    63
Michigan, 32,33,39,83
Michilimackinac, 63
Mide, 91
Miere or Walk in Water,
    35
Milford, 99
Milhametche, 45
Mill Creek, 10
Ming, John or Hoomaurow,
    57
Mingoes, 49,56,73,75,87
Mingo Village, 69,70
Minguas, 55
Minor, Peter or Yellow Hair,
    65
Mississippi River, 39,40,46,
    47,51,54,61,62,63,65,
    81,90,98
Missouri, 57
Missouri River, 39
Misquacoonacaw or Red Pole,
    44
Moautaau, 38
Mobile River, FL, 41
Mohawks, 26,48,92

Mohican, 82
Mohican Johnstown,
    69,73
Molasses, 50
Mondushawquaw, 38
Monque, 74
Monroe Twp., 67
Montgomery, Charles, 95
Montgomery County, 20
Montour, Andrew, 95
Montour, Billy or
    Hawdorowwatistie,
    57,69
Montour's Point, 95
Montreal, 33,88
Moore, William, 104
Moravian Mission,
    56,73,79
Moses, 57
Mounds, 14,15,16,17,19,
    20,23,25
Mound Builders, 14,15,
    16,17,18,19,20,
    21,22,23,24,25
Mugwaymanotreka, 45
Muccotaipeenaisco, 65
Muckquiona or Bear-
    skin, 65
Munsee, 32,40,54,55,
    62
Murray, Capt., 69
Muskingum River, 55,56,
    57,66,78,79
Myatousha, 38

Naatoua, 38
Nacudseoranauaurayk,
    38
Nadocays, 38
Nagohquagogh or
    LeGris, 61
Nahanexa, 50
Namepich or Carp, 63
Nanabosho, 92
Nanticoke, James, 57
Narowayshaus, 38
Nartekah, 45
Nashawtoomons, 38

Naskaka, 45
Nauquagasheek, 65
Nautennee, 38
Nawanaunonelo, 38
Nawaushea, 61
Nawcatay, 38
Nawebesheco or White
    Feather, 45
Nawsottomaugh, 38
Nawwene, 50
Nayau, 50
Naynuhanky, 38
Necoshecu, 45
Negro Point, 37
Nekakeka, 45
Nekeik or Little Otter, 65
Nelson's Station, 102
Nemecashe, 45
Nepaho, 45
Nequakabuchka, 46
Nequatren, 50
Nequetanghaw, 44
Nernpeneshequah or Corn-
    stalk, 45,77
Neshaustay, 38
Neslauuta, 50
Netahopuna, 57
Neudooslau, 38
Neuters, 48
Newahetucca, 45
Newark, 17,95
New Boston, 67
Newdeetoutow, 38
Newell, Joseph, 39
New Spain, 41
Newtauyaro, 50
Newville, 69
New Year's Festival, 91
New York, 48
Niagara River, 26,27,48
Nianymseka, 44
Nicholas or Orontony, 33
Nondaiwau, 65
Noon or Miaghqua, 61
Noriyettete, 38
Norrorow, 38
Northampton, 70
Notawas, 61

Nugent, Rachel, 37
Nynoah, 50

Oahashe, 46
Odell's Mill, 96
Ogonse, 65
Oharrowtodee or
    Turning Over,
    50
Oharvatoy, 38
Ohawee, 45
Ohio, ii,1,32,33,34
Ohio Valley, i,34
Ohio River, 26,42,62,
    71,75,95
Ohipwah, 45
Ohoutautoon, 38
Old Chillicothe,
    66,67,70,77
Olden, ----, 103
Old Foot or Tayouonte,
    50
Omaumeg, 59
Omitztseshaw, 38
Omussenau, 65
Onawaskine, 46
Ondewaus, 38
One Eyed Prophet, 88
Oneidas, 26,48,92
Onondaga Hollow, 27
Onondagas, 26,28,
    48,92
Onowaskemo or Resol-
    ute Man, 45
Opessah, Chief, 41
Oquainaasa, 65
Oquanoxa's Village, 65
Oquasheno or Joe, 49
Orawhaotodie or
    Turn Over, 50
Oreroimo or Little
    Fox, 46
Orontony or Nicholas,
    33
Osage, 65
Osas, 61
Oschano or Charlo,
    65
Oshawwanon, 65
Oshoquene, 65
Oshoutoy or Burning Berry,
    50
Oswego River, 27
Otharasa or Yellow, 45
Othawakeseka or Yellow
    Feather, 44
Ottawas River, 33,44,63
Ottawa, 32,35,40,47,54,58,
    62,63,64,65,70,88,
    94
Ottawa Village, 70,79
Owawtatuu, 38
Owl, 50

Paahmehelot, 57
Pachetah, 45
Paddling or Howyouway, 50
Pahaweou, 46
Paint Creek, 20,67
Pamathawwah or George
    Williams, 46
Pamoxet or Armstrong,
    57
Pamthee or Walker, 45
Panhoar, 45
Pantee, 65
Papppellelond or Beaver
    Hat, 57
Papskeecha or Flat
    Belly, 61
Parks, Billy or
    Lawnoetuchu, 46
Parks, Joseph or Joso, 46
Peacock, 39
Peaitchta, 46,87
Peaseca or Wolf, 45
Peconbequa or Woman
    Striking, 61
Peejeewa or Richardville,
    61
Peetah or Davy Baker, 45
Peeththa or Falling Tree,
    45
Pelaculbe, 45
Pelaske, 45
Peliska, 46

Pemata, 45
Pemthala or John Perry, 44
Pemthewtew or John Perry, 45
Penaiswe, 65
Penaiswonquet, 65
Penitchthamtah or Peter Cornstalk, 45
Penn, William, 41,55,78
Pennsylvania, 48,56,69,75
Peoria, 61
Pepacoshe, 46
Pepicokia, 59
Pereacumme, 45
Perrot, 59
Perry or Lullaway or Alawemetahuck, 45
Perry County, 66
Perry, John or Pemthewtew, 45
Perry, John or Pemthala, 44
Perry, William or Kayketchheka, 45
Peshawa or Richardville, 61
Peshekeinee, 65
Pesheto, 45
Petchaka, Elizabeth, 57
Petchenanalas, 57
Petersburg, 97
Peters, Isaac, 44
Petonoquet, 65
Peyamawksey, 56
Philadelphia, 72,78
Phoeniz, 67
Pht or Fallen Timbers, 87
Piankashaws, 32,40,54,58,59,62

Pickaway County, 44,67
Pickawillany, 59
Pickerington, 66
Pike County, 67
Pipe, Capt. or Tahunqacoppi, 57,69,73,74,96,97
Pipe, Eli, 57
Piqua, 42,44,59,66,67,71,75,76,77,81,83,84
Pittsburg, PA, 71,98
Plain City, 34
Planting Festival, 91
Playful, 50
Pleasant Valley Station, 103
Pochecaw, 45
Poe, Adam, 34
Poe, Andrew, 34
Point, 102
Point Pleasant, 44,77
Polk, 98
Pomthe or Walker, 44
Pontiac, 48,63,65,94
Ponty, 70
Portage County, 69
Potawatomi, 32,40,47,54,58,62,63,88
Presque Isle, 79,83,87
Prophet or Ellskwatawa or Laulewasikau, 81
Prophet's Town, 89
Pryor, Andrew, 103
Pryor, Moses, 103
Puckconsittond, 57
Pucksekaw, 42
Pukeesheno, 81
Punch, George or T. Undetaso or Teoudetass, 38,39
Punchhuck or Capt. Beaver, 57
Pushmataha, 81

Quacint, 65
Quacowawnee, 45
Quahaho, 45
Quahethu, 45
Quaker Mission, 77

Quaker Run, 77
Quakers, 41
Quanako, 45
Quaskee or Quasky, 45,72
Quebec, 88
Quesdaska, 46
Quelaoshu, 46
Quelawe, 45
Quellime, 46
Quenaghtootmait, 57
Queskhawksey or George Washinton, 57
Quequesaw, 50
Quilna, 46
Quouqua, 39

Raccoon Creek, 67
Raccoontown, 67
Rahisaus, 38
Rainbow, 91
Ramuye or Hold the Sky, 50
Ranken, James, 38,39
Rapids of the Miami, 40,47,54,57,62
Ratliff, ----, 95
Razor, 38
Reading, 104
Red Feather or Maghpiway, 56
Red Hawk, 42,77,78
Red Pole or Misquacoonacaw, 42
Red River, 57
Red Skin, 50
Restone, PA, 103
Reed, Capt., 45
Reed, Ebenezer Z., 39
Renappi, 55
Rentueco, 56
Resolute Man or Onowaskemo, 45
Rewauyeato or Carrying the News, 50

Richardville or Peejeewa, 61
Richardville, Chief Jean Baptiste, 61
Richardville, Joseph, 61
Richardville, Joseph Jr., 61
Richland County, 22,69,70, 74
Richmond, 86
Rique, 26,31
Rivarre, Antoine, 61
Robb, David, 46
Robertaile, Robert, 39
Robin or Skilleway, 45,49
Roenunas, 39
Rontayau, 35
Rontondee, 35
Ronunaise or Wiping Stick, 50
Roosayn, 38
Ross County, 14,20
Roudootouk, 38
Roudouma or Sap Running, 50
Roueyoutacolo, 38
Roughleg, 50
Roumelay, 38
Round Bottom, 99
Roundhead, 72,73
Round the Point or Taongauats, 50
Rumskaka or Kumskaukau, 81
Running About, 49,50

Sacachewa, 45
Sadowerrais, 38
Sadudeto, 50
Sage, Mrs. 95
Saharosor, 38
St. Clair, ----, 56, 71,77, 79
St. John's, 71
St. Joseph River, 59,83
St. Lawrence River, 33,41,48
St. Mary's, 40,41,54,58,61, 62,84
St. Mary's River, 65,83

Sam or Shoma, 45
Samendue or Capt. Sigore, 49
Sammy, 50
Sanders or Tapea, 45
Sandusky, 48,49,56,63, 69
Sandusky Bay, 33
Sandusky River, 35,37, 39,47,48,49,51, 57,74
Sanondoyourayquaw or Silas Armstrong, 57
Sanoreeshoe, 38
Sanorowsha, 38
Sap Running or Roudouma, 50
Sarrahoss, 38
Sarrowsauimatare or Striking Sword, 50
Sasakuthka or Sun, 61
Saudaurous or Split the River, 50
Saudotoss, 38
Sauratoudo or William Zane, 38
Sauyounaoskra, 38
Savannah, 98
Sawacotu or Yellow Clouds, 45
Sawaronuis, 38
Sawgamaw, 65
Sawyourawot, 38
Schowondashres, 38
Scioto, 70
Scioto River, 34,41, 42,44,67,72,77
Scioto Valley, 10,20, 22
Scippo Creek, 67
Scotash, 34
Scoutash, 38
Scowneti, 50
Secaw, 63
Seneca, 26,27,28,31,33, 37,40,47,48,49,50, 51,62,87,92,95

Seneca Lake, 27,48
Seneca Steel, 51
Seneca Village, 70
Sennewdorow, 38
Sentumass, 38
Serpent of Great Lakes, 91
Serroymuch, 38
Sequate, 50
Sewapen, 45
Seward, James, 103
Shaawrunthe, 35
Shacosaw, 50
Shake the Ground, 50
Shamadeesay, 38
Shamekunnesa or Soldier, 61
Shane, Anthony, 65
Shaneetown, 67
Shapukaha, 45
Shateyyaronyah or Leather Lips, 35
Shaudauaye, 38
Shauromou, 38
Shawdouyeayourou, 38
Shawnaha, 46
Shawnees, 10,32,34,40,41,42, 43,44,45,46,47,54,58, 59,62,66,67,70,71,72, 77,78,81,83,84,86,87, 88
Shawneetown, 87
Shawnetaurew, 38
Shealawhe, 45
Shealewarron, 45
Sheatwah, 45
Shekaghkela or Turtle, 45
Shekoghkell or Big Turtle, 49
Shemakib, 45
Shemanita or Snake, 45
Shemenetoo or Big Snake, 44
Sheperkiscoshe, 45
Shesecopea, 46
Shesholou, 45
Shetouyouwee or Sweet Foot, 50
Shiawa or John Solomon, 39

Shicho, 45
Shikellimus or Shikel-
  lamy, 75
Shinagawmashe, 46
Shingess or Buckonga-
  helas, 78,79
Shoma or Sam, 45
Showweno, 38
Shuagunme, 45
Sieutinque, 50
Sigore, Capt. or Sam-
  endue, 49
Silochaheca, 45
Silver, 50
Simcoe, Gov., 80
Sinamahon or Stone
  Eater, 61
Sinnecowacheckowe
  or Leek, 50
Sioux, 63
Sippo Creek, 44
Six Nations, 55,59
Siyarech, 38
Skahomet or Black
  Chief, 35
Skapoawah or George
  McDongal, 45
Skashowaysquaw, 38
Skawduutoutee, 38
Skekacumpskekaw, 45
Skekoghkell or Big
  Turtle, 51
Skeletons, 15,20,22
Skilleway or Robin, 49
Skilowa or Robin, 45
Skoutous, 39
Slippery Nose, 50
Small Cloud Spicer, 51
Smalley, William, 79
Smith, Capt., 49,50
Smith, John, 50
Snake or Shemanita, 45
Soldier or Shamekun-
  nesa, 61
Solomon, John or Shiawa, 39
Sonontouan, 48
Soomodowot, 38

Sootonteeree, 38
Sootreeshuskoh, 38
Spicer, William, 49
Spike Buck, 50
Split the River or Sau-
  daurous, 50
Sports, 8
Springer's Spring, 70
Springfield, 44,67,73
Springfield Twp., 103
Squataugh, 38
Squaw Town, 44
Squeendehtee, 39
Squindatee, 38
Standing Bones, 50
Standing Stone, 50,69
Station Spring, 103
Stayetah, 35
Steubenville, 35
Stewart, Nancy, 45,80
Stiahta, 72
Stigwanish, 70
Stone Eater or Sinamahon, 61
Stone Pestles, 23
Stone Relics, 23
Strawberry Festival, 91
Striking Sword or
  Sarrowsauismatare, 50
Stripping the River or
  Haudonwauays, 50
Suchusque, 50
Summitt County, 22,69,70
Sun or Saskuthka, 61
Susain, 65
Susannah, 38
Sutteasee, 50
Suthemoore, 50
Suyouturaw, 38
Swanendael, 55
Swedes, 55
Sweet Foot or Shetouyouwee, 50
Syhrundash, 38
Symmes, Judge, 101
Symmes Purchase, 99
Syunout or Give It to Her, 50

Syuwasautau, 50
Syuwewataugh, 38

Tahautoshowweda, 38
Tahawshodeuyea, 38
Tahawmadoyaw, 49
Tahocayn, 50
Tahoroudoyou or
   Two, 38
Tahawquevouws, 38
Tahorowtsemdee, 38
Tahorroshoquaw, 38
Tahowmandoyou, 50
Tahowtoorams or Jo
   Smee, 50
Tahunehawettee or
   Adam Brown, 35
Tahunqeccoppi or
   Capt. Pipe, 57
Tail's End or Chak-
   alowah, 44
Tall Chief or Isoh-
   auhasay, 50
Tall Man, 50
Tamataurank, 38
Tanorawayout, 38
Taongauats or Round
   the Point, 50
Tapea or Sanders, 45
Tapesheka, 45
Tarhe or Crane, 35
Tarsduhatse or Large
   Bones, 50
Tasauk, 50
Tashishee, 45
Tashmwa, 65
Tathtenouga, 61
Tatrarow, 38
Tauhaugainstoany
   Holding His
   Hand About, 50
Tauhunsequa, 50
Taunerowyea or Two
   Companies, 50
Tauomatsaarau, 38
Tauoodowma, 38
Tauosanays, 38
Tauosanetee, 50

Tauroonee, 39
Taurowtotucawaa, 38
Taushaushaurow or Cross
   the Arms, 50
Tauslowquowsay or Twenty
   Wives, 50
Tauyau, 35
Tauyaudautauson, 35
Tauyouranuta, 38
Tauyoureehoryeow, 38
Tawareroons, 38
Tawaumanocay or E. Wright,
   38
Taweesho, 38
Tawgyou, Joseph, 49
Tawiscaron, 93
Tawtoolowme, 38
Tawwass, 38
Tawyaurontoreyea, 38
Tawyougaustayou, 38
Tayagonendagighti, 48
Tayoudrakele, 38
Tayouonte or Old Foot,
   50
Tecumseh, ii,44,73,81,82
Tecumtequa, 45
Tecutio or Gurge, 45
Tehaawtorens, 35
Tehonweghrigagi, 48
Tennery, Joseph L., 39
Tennery, William M., 39
Teorow or Black Racoon, 57
Teoudetoss or George
   Punch, 39
Tepeteseca, 45
Teshawtaugh, 38
Testeatete, 38
Tetabokshke or Grand
   Glaize King, 56
Teteeopatha, 45
Tetotu, 45
Tweightewee Town, 70
Teyyaghtaw, 35
Thacaska or David McNair,
   45
Thacatchewa, 45
Thames River, 82
Thapaeca, 45

125

Theatsheta, 45
Thebeault, Hiram, 65
Theway, 45
Thithueculu, 45
Thomas or Menonkue, 38
Thomasheshawkah, 46
Thoswa, 45
Thowonawa, 63
Three Fires, 63
Thucatrouwah or Going Up the Hill, 45
Thucusen or Jim Blue Jacket, 45
Tindell, Benoni, 57
Tindell, Solomon, 57
Tippecanoe, 73,89
Tishatahoones or Widow Armstrong, 57
Tiudee, 38
Toayttooraw, 38
Tobacco, 50,91
Tochequia or Yellow Bone, 51
Tocondusque, 50
Toharratough, 38
Toleapea, 45
Tolhomanona, 38
Tomatsahoss, 38
Tommy, Capt. or Cheahaska, 45
Tondawganie or Dog, 65
Tongue, Capt., 51
Tools, 2
Toumou, 38
Tousonecta or His Blanket Down, 51
Towntoreshaw, 38
Towordu or Big Ears, 38
Towotoyoudo or Looking at Her, 50

Trapping, 8
Trautohauweetough, 38
Trayhetou, 38
Treaty at Fort Wayne, 89
Treaty at Greenville, 59,61,69,73,74,77, 79,82,83
Treuse, 50
Trickel, Stephen, 95
Trowyoudoys or G. Hunter, 50
Truman, Major, 79
Tschauendah, 35
Tucker's Station, 103
Tunis, Capt., 57
Turn Over or Orawhaotodie, 50
Turner, Ann, 61
Turner, John, 87
Turning Over or Oharrawodee, 50
Turtle or Shekaghkela, 45
Turkey Clan, 55
Turtle Clan, 55
Tuscaroras, 26
Tuscarawas River, 34,55,56, 69
Tuscarora Town, 78
Tusqugan or McCarty, 65
Tutaw, 84,85
Twaatwaa or Crane, 59
Twenty Wives or Tauslowquowsay, 50
Twightwees, 59
Twilight or Aronzon, 61
Twin Creek, 10
Two or Tahoroudoyou, 38
Two Companies or Taunerowyea, 50
Twoittois, 59
Tayaudusont or Joshua Hendricks, 50
Tyyeakwheunohale, 38

Undauwau or Matthews, 38
Upper Piqua, 70,83
Upper Sandusky, 32,34,35,74

Urbana, 86

Vanmeter, John, 37
Venango, 48
Vessels, 12,13
Vincennes, 79,89
Virginia, 41
Voorhee's Station, 104

Wabash River, 58,81
Wabatthoe, 56
Wabepee or White
    Color, 45
Waghkonoxie or White
    Bone, 51
Wakawuxsheno or
    White Man, 49
Walam Olum, 55
Walker or Pomthe or
    Pamthee, 44
Walker, Catharine, 37
Walker, Henry Clay, 39
Walker, Isaiah, 39
Walker, Joel, 39
Walker, John R., 37
Walker, John T., 39
Walker, Matthew R., 39
Walker, William, 39
Walk in the Water
    or Miere, 35
Walupe, 45
Wapakonetta, 40,44,45,
    46,71,76,77,80,
    81,83,84,86,90
Wapamangwe or White
    Loon, 61
Wapapeska, 61
Wapatha, 41
Wapeminskink, 57
Wapeskekahothew, 46
War Chief, 45
War of 1812, 11,90
War Mallet, 57
War Pole or Runtunda, 37,39

Warren County, 19
Wasagashick, 65
Wasawotah or Bright Horn, 45
Washington, DC, 47,51
Washington, George, 78,79
Washington, George or
    Queshawksey, 57
Washington, James, 39
Wathethewela or Bright
    Horn, 76,77
Waubegakake, 65
Wawelame, 45
Wawlepesshecco, 45
Waymatalhaway, 46
Wayne, Gen., 45,74,77,
    79,84
Waytheah or Long Shanks, 44
Wayweleapy, 86
Wea, 32,40,54,58,59,62
Wearecah, 45
Wells, Jane Turner, 61
Wells, Mary, 61
Wells, William Wayne, 61
Wemetche or Crescent, 61
Wendot, 33
Werewela, 45
Weythapamattha, 44
Weyapiersenwaw or Blue
    Jacket, 42,44,45,79,80
Weywinquis or Billy Siscomb, 57
When You Are Tired Sit
    Down or Willaqua-
    sheno, 49
Whirlwind or Aweallesa, 57
Whitaker, Elizabeth, 35,37
White, Jacob Capt., 103
White Bone or Waghkonoxie, 51
White Color or Wabeepee, 45
White Eyes, Capt. or
    Wicocalind, 56
Whites Eyes or Apacahund, 57

White Feather or Nawebesheco, 45
White Lion or Wapamangwa, 61
White Man or Wakawuxsheno, 49
White River, IN, 33
White's Station, 103, 104
Whitewater & Miami Valley Pioneer Assoc., 102
Wicocalind or Capt. White Eyes, 56
Wigwams, 1,2
Wild Duck, 50
Willaquasheno or When You Are Tired Sit Down, 49
Williams, Abraham, 38
Williams, George or Pamathawwah, 38,46,57
Williams, Isaac, 37,38
Williams, J., Jr., 35
Williams, Joseph, 37
Williams, Rachel, 37
Williams, Sarah, 37
Williamson, Col., 73
Winans, Lewis, 103
Winemac, 76
Winnebagoes, 89
Winpe, 94
Wiping Stick or Ronunaise, 50
Wiping Stick or Sacoureweeghta, 49,51
Wishemaw, 45
Wobby, Isaac, 57
Wockachaalli, 67
Wolf or Byaseka, 44
Wolf or Peaseca, 45
Wolf Clan, 55
Wolf, Capt., 57
Wolf, Henry Clay, 83
Wolf, John or Lawatucheh, 45,83

Wolf Rapid, 65
Woman Striking or Peconbequa, 61
Women, 2,3,4
Woolyhead, 50
Wooster, 97
Workman, D. M., 46
Wottondt or John Hicks, 38
Wright, E. or Tawaumanocay, 38
Wyandots or Hurons, 3,10,27, 32,33,34,35,36,37,38, 39,40,41,44,47,48,54, 55,58,62,67,72,73,88

Xenia, 44,66,70,86

Yellow or Otharasa, 45
Yellow Bone or Tochequia, 51
Yellow Clouds or Athelwakesoca, 45
Yellow Clouds or Sawacotu, 45
Yellow Feather or Othawakeseka, 44
Yellow Hair or Peter Minor, 65
Youausha, 38
Youdorast, 57
Youheno, 50
Youhreo, 38
Yourahatsa, 38
Youronocay or Isaac, 50
Youronurays, 38
Yourowon, 38
Yourowquains or Widow of the Crane, 38
Youshindauyato, 38
Youtradowwonlee, 50
Youwautowtoyou or Burnt His Body, 50
Youwaydauyea or the Island, 50

Zane, Ebenezer or Hayanoise, 38

Zane, William or
      Sauratoudo,
      38
Zanesville, 66
Zeisberger, Brother
      David, 56
Zeshauau or James
      Armstrong, 57

www.ingramcontent.com/pod-product-compliance
Lightning Source LLC
Chambersburg PA
CBHW070454090426
42735CB00012B/2554